THE GREAT JAZZ DRUMMERS

By Ron Spagnardi
Edited By William F. Miller

Special thanks to William F. Miller, Scott Bienstock,
Isabel Spagnardi, Adam Budofsky, Karen Walsh,
Hank O'Hara, and Chris Otazo, for their assistance
and suggestions in the preparation of this book.

Cover Photo By Ron Spagnardi

Published by: Modern Drummer Publications, Inc.
12 Old Bridge Road
Cedar Grove, New Jersey 07009-1288 U.S.A.

Table Of Contents

Introduction

I t's been our firm belief for many years at *Modern Drummer* that every serious student of drumming should have an understanding of, and an appreciation for, the rich heritage of the art form. Our primary purpose in publishing this text is to present to drummers a reference source that would offer a real sense of that heritage, while at the same time pay tribute to those artists who shaped and molded our history.

The Great Jazz Drummers looks back on nearly a century of drumming activity. The 62 drummer profiles that follow offer an accurate perspective of how the story has unfolded—a story that began during the '20s in New Orleans, progressed through the legendary big band drummers of the '30s, the bop pioneers of the '40s and '50s, and the '60s and '70s free stylists and fusionists, and continues with the great players of today who have brought the art to such a high level.

Each of the individual profiles contained here offers not only biographical information, but also attempts to pinpoint the artist's style, his contribution to drumming, and the overall extent of his influence on other players. In some cases that information was culled from a player's own vivid recollections, and in other cases through the words of colleagues.

We believe the inclusion of the Sound Supplement makes *The Great Jazz Drummers* a valuable listening experience as well as a literary one. The 16 important players presented on the recording represent a period of roughly seven decades, and demonstrate the gradual progression of jazz drumming from one generation to the next. Clearly, there's a bloodline that runs from Baby Dodds to Jack DeJohnette, from Papa Jo to Tony Williams. And though that bloodline may at times appear blurred, there is certainly no doubting its existence.

As you work your way through this volume, hopefully you'll come away with a better understanding and a greater appreciation for the rich tradition of the art of jazz drumming. Of course, along with that understanding and appreciation, we hope you'll find the journey back in time through *The Great Jazz Drummers* a rewarding and fascinating experience, as well.

Ron Spagnardi
Editor/Publisher
Modern Drummer Publications

Arthur "Zutty" Singleton

Zutty Singleton was born in Bunkie, Louisiana in 1898, and was basically a self-taught drummer. During his illustrious career he worked with Steve Louis, The Tuxedo Jazz Band, Louis Nelson, The Maple Leaf Band, and the popular Fate Marable. However, Singleton would not gain national recognition until his recordings with Louis Armstrong's Hot Five were made during the '20s.

In 1917, Singleton was part of the migration of jazz musicians to Chicago, where jazz activity was flourishing. While there, he performed with Doc Cook, Dave Payton, and Jimmie Noone, and later in New York with Armstrong, Fats Waller, and Sidney Bechet. He also recorded with Pee Wee Russell, Jelly Roll Morton, Wingy Manone, and Buster Bailey.

Known for his great suppleness, Singleton followed the melodic lines of a jazz improvisation more closely than anyone who had come before. He also utilized a more modest setup in comparison to other drummers of his era. With the exception of the standard novelty effects, Singleton limited himself to a snare drum, bass drum, two toms, and two or three cymbals.

"When we soloed," recalled Singleton, "we had all kinds of gimmicks—skillets, ratchets, bells, Chinese toms, Chinese cymbals—everything. But there was very little rhythmic syncopation. All you had to do was keep good time."

Another key element of Singleton's style was his use of the snare drum press roll accentuated on the second and fourth beats to maintain the pulse. Singleton's press roll timekeeping technique was actually the forerunner of the modern jazz cymbal beat.

"The first pair of brushes I ever had were given to me by Louis Cotrelle," said Singleton. "I studied Cotrelle's work a lot during the early days. But Louis didn't care about brushes, so he gave them to me. They were the first pair of brushes I ever saw in my life. Before that, you had to get your soft effects by controlling your touch with the sticks."

In 1974, Singleton was awarded the Gene Krupa Award, and in 1975 he was voted into the NARAS Hall Of Fame for his performances on the Louis Armstrong Hot Five recordings that were made in 1928. A stroke rendered Singleton inactive in 1969, and he died in New York in '75. Fans of traditional jazz continue to rank Arthur "Zutty" Singleton as a true jazz drumming pioneer and a leader in the field.

**"We just kept the rhythm going and hardly ever took a solo."
—Zutty Singleton**

Warren "Baby" Dodds

Warren "Baby" Dodds was born in New Orleans, Louisiana in 1898, and studied drums with Dave Perkins, Walter Brundy, Henry Zeno, and Louis Cotrelle. His playing career began with Willie Hightower and Papa Celestin, and on Mississippi riverboats with Fate Marable. In 1921, Dodds joined the famous King Oliver Creole Jazz Band in Chicago with fellow sideman Louis Armstrong, and soon became the most influential jazz drummer of the '20s.

After leaving Oliver, Dodds worked with Freddie Keppard, Johnny Dodds, and Lil Armstrong, and later recorded with Louis Armstrong's Hot Seven. While house drummer at New York's Three Deuces from 1936 to 1939, he performed and recorded with a host of prominent jazz artists including Sidney Bechet, Jimmy Noone, Mezz Mezzrow, Bunk Johnson, Art Hodes, and Miff Mole. After suffering strokes in 1949 and '50, Dodds returned to Chicago and continued to perform there from 1952 until his retirement in '57.

Baby Dodds embodied the *spirit* and *tradition* of early military-flavored jazz. His carefully tuned drums were resonant, melodic, and harmonic. While performing at the famed Lincoln Gardens in Chicago, Dodds used a 28" bass drum, a metal snare, four cowbells, a slapstick, a woodblock, a 16" Chinese cymbal, and a 10" Chinese tom-tom. Dodds was the first jazz drummer to extract the full potential of the bass drum by making its rhythmic undercurrent the foundation of the band. His subtle playing was characterized by a smooth yet firm time feel, flavored with crackling press rolls.

Baby Dodds is credited with being one of the first drummers to play breaks and fills between phrases and solos. And though simplistic by today's standards, they marked the beginning of the drum solo itself. Dodds was also one of the first to convert the press roll time pattern to the basic ride cymbal beat used today. And while he adhered to a military style of drumming throughout most of his career, it was his acute sense of pitch, subtlety, and rhythmic inventiveness that bridged the gap between the strict military structure, and the freer, more *flowing* style that would soon emerge.

Finally, Dodds was among the first to totally interact with the ensemble through changes in patterns and textures. "I was struck with the range and constant shifting of tonal colors Baby displayed as he moved all over his set," said Max Roach. "He continued to vary the sound of his beat according to the soloist."

With a style that has had an impact on virtually hundreds of other drummers since the early '20s, Warren "Baby" Dodds has rightfully earned his place in music history as the world's *first* great jazz drummer.

"Dodds was swingin' so much, I was late an entire set. But I couldn't leave. I sat down and just stayed."
—Philly Joe Jones

"Baby taught me more than all the others. He was the first great soloist."
—Gene Krupa

George Wettling

Strongly influenced by Baby Dodds, George Wettling became one of the leading proponents of the early "Chicago style" of jazz drumming. A tasteful, imaginative, unobtrusive drummer, Wettling quickly built a reputation as the ultimate band player. Though the few solos he took were inventive and well-conceived, Wettling's primary interest was in functioning as a solid accompanist where the *music* came before everything else.

George Wettling was born in Topeka, Kansas in 1907 and raised in Chicago. He began his professional career in 1924 with a host of local bands, and made his first recordings with the Jungle Kings in 1927. Shortly after, he took Dave Tough's place with the Chicago Wolverines. George arrived in New York in 1935, and over the years worked with Louis Panico, Wingy Manone, Artie Shaw, Bunny Berrigan, Joe Marsala, Red Norvo, and Eddie Condon. Though unfairly stereotyped as a strong small-group player, Wettling was equally at home in a large-band setting as well, performing with big bands led by Charlie Barnet, Johnny Long, Woody Herman, and Paul Whiteman. A highly skilled, well-educated player, Wettling also held the drum chair with ABC Radio from 1943 to 1952, though his attachment to jazz prompted him to also lead his own band around the New York area throughout the early '50s.

George Wettling took the conceptual and stylistic elements of Baby Dodds and brought them to the next level. Though the predominant "four beat" bass drum always remained a Wettling trademark, his style also included the addition of color and shading, a firm yet supple time feel, and a delicate touch. Blending *with* the band, as opposed to standing apart from it, was his major musical concern. Though unjustly underrated among jazz historians, George Wettling was an important link between the ground-breaking work of Baby Dodds, and the more advanced approach taken by Dave Tough and Gene Krupa. Wettling died in New York City in June of 1968.

> "There are other drummers with a sure sense of time, but George was absolutely dependable. If a band had George behind it, it knew it had some strength."
> —Eddie Condon

Sonny Greer

"Sonny knew what audiences liked," said Mercer Ellington. "He was one of the few people from whom Duke readily took advice. A great reactor to material, he needed only a skeleton of an idea. With that as a base, he'd contribute a great deal to the glory of a work. Sonny had a great ear and unusual reflexes."

Born in 1903 in Long Branch, New Jersey, Sonny Greer studied drums with vaudeville drummer J. Rosmond Johnson. His first professional job was as a youngster in a pit band in Red Bank, New Jersey. Within a few years, he was working in the pit orchestra at the Plaza Hotel in Asbury Park. While at the Plaza, Greer met Duke Ellington and the two began performing together in Ellington's hometown of Washington, DC. It was the beginning of an association that ran from 1923 to 1951.

Greer's stay with the Ellington band reached a pinnacle during their years at New York's legendary Cotton Club. A distinctive, musical drummer, Greer was noted for his elaborate drumset, which was so impressive, special mention of it was made in Jim Haskin's book *The Cotton Club*: "Greer and his drums provided the focus of the band's music. He had an incredible battery of percussion equipment. Everything from tom-toms to snare and kettle drums. And once he realized the band was at the club to stay awhile, he brought in the really good stuff. Sonny later recalled: 'When we got into The Cotton Club, presentation became very important. I was a designer for the Leedy Company, and the president had a fabulous set of drums made for me with timpani, chimes, vibraphone—everything. Musicians used to come to The Cotton Club just to see it. The value of it was $3000, a lot of money at that time.' With such equipment, Greer could make every possible drum sound, and at The Cotton Club he awed the customers, conjuring up tribal warriors, man-eating tigers, and war dancers."

Along with being a great showman, Sonny Greer was acknowledged for his natural ability and excellent musical instincts. He was even known to use timpani heads on his bass drum so the drum could be tuned to a precise pitch. Greer has also been credited as being an important part of the character of the Ellington orchestra during its heyday. Sonny Greer passed away in 1982 at the age of 79.

"Back then, if you were a lame player, you'd have a hard time. But if you could play, they'd come to see you. And they'd tell you if you could play!"
—Sonny Greer

Ray Bauduc

S trongly influenced by both Baby Dodds and Zutty Singleton, Ray Bauduc was Singleton's counterpart in the white Dixieland revival. His style was an intriguing combination of vaudeville, ragtime, and the basic New Orleans rhythms he'd grown up absorbing.

Born in New Orleans in 1909, Bauduc studied drumming with Kid Peterson, a prominent New Orleans teacher. A natural drummer, Bauduc advanced rapidly and made his recording debut in 1926 at the age of 17 with The Memphis Five. In 1927 he joined the Freddy Rich Orchestra in New York, and later toured Europe with the band. However, it wasn't until 1929—as a member of the Ben Pollack band—when Bauduc truly began to develop and hone his own inimitable style.

After leaving Pollack, Bauduc joined Bob Crosby & the Bobcats, the band in which he would gain recognition as a *key* force in jazz drumming. A popular figure in the Crosby band, Bauduc was a skilled, fiery soloist who knew how to combine showmanship with musicality. Though he recorded extensively with Crosby, his most memorable effort was the hit recording of "Big Noise From Winnetka," a duet with bassist Bob Haggart where the drum solo was played on the strings of Haggart's bass. Bauduc was also known to use sticks on his bass drum, and would often play on the rims of the snare and bass drum for special effects. A loose, relaxed player, he was one of the first to utilize two small toms on the bass drum, and has also been credited with inventing a pedal tom-tom that was operated like a timpani.

Bauduc remained with the Crosby band until 1942, winning the *downbeat* award in 1940. He later went on to perform with bands led by Tommy Dorsey, Red Nichols, Benny Goodman, Joe Venuti, and Jack Teagarden. He led his own band for several years, and spent 1947-50 with Jimmy Dorsey & His Orchestra. Ray Bauduc passed away in 1988.

"He could really lay it down. Ray was loose, more like Zutty than anyone else."
—Bob Haggart

"I've never forgotten how good he was in the Bob Crosby band. A very distinctive player."
—Mel Torme

Jimmy Crawford

One of the most exciting and dynamic big bands to come out of Kansas City during the swing era was the Jimmy Lunceford band. Drummer Jimmy Crawford, a high-spirited, supportive player, was the driving force behind the Lunceford band for nearly 14 years.

Throughout the years of Lunceford's great popularity, Crawford played with a strong, solid pulsation—a classic trademark of the Lunceford sound—and was a key factor in establishing the unique Lunceford beat. Yet, like Dave Tough, his drumming was unobtrusive and always felt more than heard. Crawford could hold the band together with authority by playing heavily when the arrangement required it, yet softly and delicately when the band needed a more sensitive approach. Though never known as a particularly flashy drummer, Crawford was as solid as the Rock of Gibraltar and as reliable a drummer as any band could wish for.

Jimmy Crawford was born in 1910 in Memphis, Tennessee, and was initially influenced by Memphis drummer Booker Washington. A self-taught player, Crawford was discovered by Lunceford when the drummer was 18, and Lunceford put him in the drum chair of his hot young band in 1928. After leaving the Lunceford band in '42, Crawford worked with small groups led by Ben Webster and clarinetist Edmond Hall at New York's Cafe Society. He also played with the bands of Fletcher Henderson, Harry James, and Stan Kenton.

By the early '50s, after the majority of big bands had faded from the scene, Crawford maintained a career as a fine Broadway pit drummer. For years he remained active in such Broadway hits as *Golden Boy, Bye Bye Birdie, Mr. Wonderful,* and *Pal Joey,* among others. Always in demand, Crawford also went on to record with Count Basie, Sy Oliver, Bing Crosby, Benny Goodman, Dizzy Gillespie, and Frank Sinatra.

Jimmy Crawford died in 1980 at the age of 70 after a successful career as one of the most versatile drummers to ever grace the music scene.

**"Craw had great spirit. He consistently picked the band up. He was the driving force."
—Trummy Young**

William "Cozy" Cole

Cozy Cole, an incredibly adept player, was strongly rooted in the rudimental style, but he contributed much to jazz drumming. One of the first players to develop his own brand of hand and foot coordination, he mastered the technique thoroughly, performing solos more complex than anything that had previously been done. Cole was also known for playing four different rhythmic figures at one time (figures often divided between straight 8ths and triplets), giving the effect of two drummers playing simultaneously. His experimentation with coordinated independence was way ahead of its time, and previewed the bop drumming style of the '40s.

Cole was born in East Orange, New Jersey in 1909, and began drumming at the age of five. Though influenced by Chick Webb, Gene Krupa, and Jo Jones, Cole was initially inspired by Sonny Greer. By 1930, he was recording with Jelly Roll Morton, and shortly thereafter went on to play with Benny Carter, Stuff Smith, and Willie Bryant.

Cole achieved national prominence between 1939 and '42 in Cab Calloway's band, where he was featured on legendary recordings like "Crescendo In Drums," "Paradiddle Joe," and "Ratamacue." After the Calloway years, he worked and recorded with Lionel Hampton, Coleman Hawkins, Roy Eldridge, Jonah Jones, and Louis Armstrong's All Stars, and in 1945 he recorded with Charlie Parker and Dizzy Gillespie. Cole also worked on Broadway, and was one of the first black musicians hired as a staff player by CBS radio. During the '50s, his recording of "Topsy, Part 1" was a nationwide hit, one of only a handful of drummer-recorded hits.

Bob Breithaupt, percussion instructor at Capital University in Ohio, recalls Cozy Cole: "What he did between his hi-hat and bass drum were primarily tap dancing things. Then he'd simply play on top of it. But during the '30s, that was pretty significant because *no one* was doing it. His solo techniques were really amazing. He found he could superimpose rhythms on top of one another and get some real interesting sounds. He obviously had some coordination that most people *didn't* have."

Continually working towards personal improvement, Cole later studied snare drum with Billy Gladstone, mallets with Fred Albright, and timpani with Saul Goodman at the Juilliard School. In 1954 he opened a school for drummers with Gene Krupa and built a solid reputation as an instructor, with Philly Joe Jones among his many students. Late in his life, Cole even studied for a music degree at Capital University, one of his lifelong goals. Cozy Cole died in 1981 and remains one of jazz drumming's most important figures.

> "Cozy's contribution was a technical one: hand and foot independence. He was one of the first—if not the first—to develop and master it."
> —Don DeMichael

"Papa" Jo Jones

It's been said that modern drumming made its first step towards maturity when Jo Jones arrived in New York in 1936 with the Count Basie band. Within a few years, Jones became the idol of hundreds of drummers across the country who emulated the style he had perfected.

Born in Chicago in 1911, Jones toured with carnival bands during the late '20s, and played with some of the leading territory bands in the Midwest, including the Benny Moten band. After Moten's death in '35, Jones worked in St. Louis briefly before joining a young Count Basie at the Reno Club in Kansas City. It was within the framework of the Basie band from 1936 to 1948 where Jo Jones would make his indelible mark on the *entire* jazz drumming world.

The importance of Jones' contribution to the evolution of jazz drumming was more conceptual than technical. His natural, flowing ride cymbal beat outswung that of every predecessor, and he was a master at punctuating and underlining the figures in an arrangement. Though Jones maintained a steady-four bass drum, he began the trend of breaking up the rhythm behind soloists by dropping bass drum "bombs." He explored the tonal possibilities and dynamics of the instrument, and improved on the dry, tight sound of drummers who had come before with a relaxed, *looser* concept. He's also credited with making lasting changes in the drumset itself, discarding many of the accessories that had been used previously. He reduced the size of the bass drum, tuned his drums open and unmuffled, and used the hi-hat in a manner no one had ever thought to use it before.

More than any other drummer in history, Jo Jones developed the hi-hat into an instrument of great rhythmic and tonal variety. His hi-hat style has been characterized as swinging and driving, but never obtrusive. Early recordings with the Basie band clearly reveal a smooth, uplifting hi-hat that emphasized a longer, more *open* sound. The result was a feeling of great forward momentum that lent itself perfectly to the character and rhythmic flow of the Basie band.

Jo Jones injected relaxation, elegance, humor, and impeccable taste in his drumming, and could easily inspire an entire band with a simple, perfectly placed fill. A team player not given to displays of virtuosity, Jones was also a master of brush playing and the essence of subtlety and understatement.

More than any drummer who had come before, Jo Jones pointed drummers towards a more *musical* way of thinking about the instrument. His contributions have placed him high among the great jazz drummers of all time, and have earned him the respect of musicians from every school.

"Jo Jones swung a whole generation with the hi-hat."
—Jake Hanna

"I loved what Jo did and how he felt."
—Buddy Rich

"If you had to choose one guy—it would be Jo Jones."
—Louie Bellson

William "Chick" Webb

Possibly one of the most gifted players in jazz drumming history, Chick Webb had a significant effect on Gene Krupa, Buddy Rich, Dave Tough, Jo Jones, Sid Catlett, and many others who were all in some way influenced by his remarkable performances.

Webb was born in Baltimore in 1907, and after arriving in New York in 1924, he formed his own band and worked at places like The Cotton Club, Roseland, and The Strand Roof. However, he didn't truly gain national prominence until his band began to perform regularly at Harlem's Savoy Ballroom. Soon, word of his astounding ability circulated among drummers across the country, and Chick Webb was on his way to becoming one of the most dynamic figures in jazz.

A powerful and explosive player with magnificent control of bass drum and cymbals, Webb was both a superb soloist and an ensemble player. His unique style was more *legato* and flowing than other drummers of the day, and was a perfect blending of the military and jazz styles. Webb was also one of the first drummers to really *integrate* the drummer into the overall performance.

A tiny, hunchback man who endured much suffering throughout his career, Webb nonetheless had total control of his music. Though famous for his exciting solos and breaks, he was also a master of shading, dynamic contrast, and pitch variation. Webb's interplay between toms, snare, and cymbals was brilliant, and his solos were conceived with intelligence and executed with bewildering speed and power. His bass drum work (four to the bar even at ferocious tempos) was distinguishable from hundreds of other drummers.

Drummer Allen Paley recalls the electricity generated by a Chick Webb performance: "What he did was *totally* unbelievable. He couldn't have been more than four feet tall. But it was no problem for him. He had strong wrists, long arms, and huge hands. Sitting up high, he'd lean over the set and hit various drums and cymbals almost without moving. He was the best natural player I ever came across. Fast, clean, and flawless, he played like a machine gun, but with enormous feeling. It was almost barbaric the way he drove that band. When he played a break, it was here and gone! You couldn't get hold of it. Yet everything fit. His comments worked as drum patterns, *and* as music. I never heard him play a bad break or solo."

Four years after discovering vocalist Ella Fitzgerald in 1935, Chick Webb died of tuberculosis at the age of 32. The band would continue for another three years before dissolving, but the impact of Chick Webb's drumming has lived on among jazz drummers the world over.

"The man could reach amazing heights. When he felt like it, he could cut down any of us."
—Gene Krupa

"If he were alive now, I think most drummers would be trying to figure out why they decided to play drums. That's how good he was. I idolized him."
◆ —Buddy Rich

J.C. Heard

J.C. Heard was born in Detroit in 1917, and started out as a tap dancer. He taught himself drums at age 11, and two years later he was working with local bands. Heard's break into the big time came in 1938 as a member of Teddy Wilson's band, formed shortly after Wilson departed from the Benny Goodman band. After the breakup of Wilson's band, J.C. worked with bands led by Benny Carter, Louis Jordan, Count Basie, Louis Armstrong, and Benny Goodman, and performed on live radio broadcasts from New York's Savoy Ballroom with Coleman Hawkins, Cab Calloway, and Woody Herman.

During the '40s, Heard appeared in several Hollywood films including *Stormy Weather* and *Boogie Woogie's Dream*, and in 1946 he received *Esquire* magazine's prestigious *Drummer Of The Year* award. He worked with Erroll Garner at The Three Dueces in '48, and later joined Norman Granz's *Jazz At The Philharmonic*, where he toured the United States and Japan. Heard also fronted his own quartet in Los Angeles, New York, and Las Vegas, played with jazz luminaries Roy Eldridge, Dizzy Gillespie, and Charlie Parker, and made appearances at most of the major European Jazz Festivals.

Heard was one of the jazz world's more personable figures, and is recognized for his masterful timekeeping and brilliant solo work. "Unless you know how to phrase, unless you have some ideas about presence, conception, and attitude, then your solos are just going to be a bunch of noise," said Heard.

In great demand throughout his career, Heard is reportedly on over 1,100 albums with various performers including Charles Mingus, Ray Brown, Charlie Parker, Billie Holiday, Ray Charles, Nat King Cole, Dinah Washington, and Sarah Vaughan. J.C. Heard reflected on his diversified and productive career in a 1988 *MD* interview: "In those days, if you couldn't play in a big band, they would write you off. It was different than it is now. I made my name as a big band drummer, as did Sid Catlett and Papa Jo, even though we all also worked with small combos. You had to do it all—and learn it all—to be good."

"I did all the first stuff with Bird and Diz. People think it was Max because the sidemen aren't listed. I was in that band before Max."
—J.C. Heard

Ray McKinley

"**M**c Kinley is the product of an era that preceded the emergence of drummers bent on showing what they could do," said drummer Cliff Leeman. "Unlike many of the highly technical drummers, McKinley combined elements of showmanship with thoughtful, feeling performances. He never ignored his timekeeping duties."

Ray McKinley was born in Fort Worth, Texas, and began playing at the age of four. Though self-taught, he was inspired to play by pit drummer Jimmy Grimes. His career began in the Fort Worth and Dallas areas with local bands, and his first major break occurred in 1926 with the Duncan-Marin band. After working with Beasley Smith in Nashville and the Tracy-Brown band in Pittsburgh, McKinley joined Milt Shaw & the Detroiters at New York's Roseland Ballroom in 1930. Shortly thereafter, he became a member of the famed Dorsey Brothers Orchestra, and after the two brothers split up, he stayed with Jimmy Dorsey until 1939. McKinley later co-led a band with Will Bradley, had his own band briefly in '42, and then joined the world-renowned Glenn Miller band. He formed his own band once again in 1945, but called it quits in '51. Unable to fully retire, he later led the revived Glenn Miller Orchestra from 1956-'66.

An extremely supportive player, McKinley possessed a natural, *flowing* time feel and was a masterful timekeeper. According to Cliff Leeman, "Krupa—whose technique and attention-getting devices were so well-developed—got the whole showboat trend going. It was a healthy thing that there were a number of drummers around like Mac, whose work reminded other drummers of what had to be done."

Jimmy Maxwell, one of McKinley's bandmates in the Dorsey band, provided another view: "Ray was great at holding the band together. He was authoritative and sensitive. And he really knew how to color and fill in the open spaces. Like Dave Tough and Sonny Greer, he seemed to come up with just the *right* figure and little touch."

Finally, Carmen Mastern, guitarist in the Miller band, fondly recalled Ray McKinley: "Mac realized that it was the rhythm section—not any *one* player—that really was important. A lot of drummers don't care about the rhythm section. They play for themselves. McKinley seldom forgot *why* he was there, and what he should do."

> "**Supposedly, timekeeping was the drummer's basic function. But too many drummers were busy doing other things.**"
> **—Ray McKinley**

Sidney "Big Sid" Catlett

Though Big Sid Catlett came out of the swing era, he is best remembered for a drumming style that had a marked influence on the bop drummers of the '40s. Catlett bridged the gap between the two genres, and his recordings with Dizzy Gillespie and Charlie Parker made him one of the few drummers to survive the transition from swing to bop.

Catlett was born in Evansville, Indiana in 1910, and began his career in Chicago at 16. After coming to New York in 1930 with Sammy Stewart, he went on to work with McKinney's Cotton Pickers, Fletcher Henderson, Benny Carter, Don Redman, Rex Stewart, and Teddy Wilson. He spent 1938-'42 with Louis Armstrong, and played with Benny Goodman's band for a short while in '41. A notable figure on the 52nd Street scene, Catlett performed with Ben Webster, Don Byas, and Lester Young, and is on countless record dates with other leading players. Winner of the *Esquire* Gold Award in 1944 and '45, he later returned to Armstrong's All Star band in 1947. The last years of his life were spent free-lancing in Chicago, where he died in March of 1951.

Like Jo Jones, Sid Catlett influenced drummers primarily for his conceptual innovations and his contribution to the rhythm section as a whole. Acclaimed for his remarkably steady timekeeping, Catlett was a functional player who believed his primary task was to *integrate* the rhythm section into the work of the entire group. Though influenced early on by Zutty Singleton's military flavor, Catlett developed a linearity that had not been heard before. An incredibly adaptable drummer, he was at home in small groups or big bands, New Orleans style to bop.

Though more of a low-profile player than his contemporaries, Catlett could be a great showman when the need arose, and he had outstanding technical ability. However, his key motivation was the music. The epitome of grace and beauty, his playing was firm, supportive, and extremely tasteful, with a great sense of form and structure. His solos were explorations of themes and variations, where melodic opening statements were set up, repeated, and then embellished. These ingeniously structured solos exemplified Catlett's *keen* sense of dynamics, humor, and surprise, beginning at times at thunderous levels and ending at delicate *pianissimos*. His bass drum explosions echoed in the early work of the modernists, and his hi-hat style helped popularize the instrument as a primary timekeeping device.

Acknowledged as an important pivotal player, Big Sid would have a direct impact on the drumming of Max Roach, Art Blakey, Shelly Manne, Stan Levey, and Ed Shaughnessy. An inspired performer, Big Sid Catlett is considered one of the most important drummers who ever lived.

> "He didn't have to be the bombastic, take-over drummer. He always was the musician."
> —Billy Taylor

> "I think he had the smoothest style of any drummer of that era and possibly since. Everything flowed."
> —Ed Shaughnessy

CLIFF LEEMAN
ARTIE SHAW'S ORCHESTRA

Cliff Leeman

"I try to play behind the soloist. I'd rather play a four-bar chase chorus with a horn, something with different tones and sounds, than get into a rudimental solo," said Cliff Leeman, one of jazz drumming's most tasteful artists.

Never the showman—therefore not well-recognized by the public—Leeman concentrated on making the band sound good and the players feel comfortable. Greatly admired by musicians, Cliff Leeman was popular in big band circles for his marvelous timekeeping and effortless swing.

Leeman was born in Portland, Maine in 1913, studied locally, and began his career in Kansas City with Murphy's Musical Skippers. Over the years he performed with many of the prominent jazz players including Eddie Condon, Red Norvo, Jimmy Rushing, Joe Venuti, Peanuts Hucko, and Teddy Wilson. In 1936, he made his mark as an important big band drummer with the Artie Shaw band, recording such great hits as "Back Bay Shuffle," and "Begin The Beguine." After leaving Shaw, he worked with Tommy Dorsey, Charlie Barnet, and the Woody Herman band, where he remained until 1944.

By the mid-'40s, Leeman had pretty much settled into the small-group mold, playing with John Kirby, Ben Webster, and Don Byas. He also toured Europe and recorded with Bobby Hackett and Wild Bill Davidson. The latter years of his career were spent in radio and recording studio work, and as drummer on the Perry Como, Jack Benny, Steve Allen, and *Your Hit Parade* TV shows.

A great admirer of Zutty Singleton, Jo Jones, and Sid Catlett, Leeman possessed a style that was the embodiment of good taste combined with an artistic, musical approach. He's also been credited with popularizing the Chinese cymbal within the big band idiom. "I played that 25" Chinese cymbal all through the big band years," said Leeman in an *MD* interview. "It became something of a trademark of mine. I used it with Shaw, Dorsey, and Charlie Barnet."

Though quite capable of playing outstanding solos, Leeman had little desire to do so. Quite content remaining in a totally supportive position, his refined sense of swing and rock-solid time uplifted every band he worked with. Cliff Leeman passed away in 1986 at the age of 73.

"Cliff left little to be desired. He never did too little, or too much."
—Pee Wee Erwin

O'Neil Spencer

S olidly rooted in the Sid Catlett school of drumming was O'Neil Spencer, a somewhat lesser-known player who nonetheless had a significant effect on the musicians he played with and the drummers who heard him.

Spencer was born in Cedarville, Ohio in 1909 and began his career with local bands in the Buffalo, New York area. In 1931, he joined up with the Mills Blue Rhythm Band, which later became the Lucky Millinder Orchestra. However, it wasn't until 1937—after he joined the popular John Kirby Sextet—that Spencer truly became an influential force on the jazz scene.

A first-class swing drummer and an exceptional stylist, Spencer was well-adapted to either a small group or big band environment. Along with being one of the finest show drummers who ever lived, he was also a superb brush player with a precise, powerful style that was quite capable of inspiring an entire band. Though never recognized as a flashy drummer, Spencer was a masterful player who performed on meticulously tuned drums in the tradition of Jo Jones, Dave Tough, and Sid Catlett.

Though he became well-known primarily through his work with John Kirby, Spencer also recorded during the late '30s with numerous other groups, including those led by Red Allen, Sidney Bechet, Jimmie Noone, Johnny Dodds, Frankie Newton, Milt Hearth, and Lil Armstrong.

Buddy Rich remembers hearing O'Neil Spencer: "I first met Spence when he was at the Onyx with the Kirby band. With those brushes, he caught the feeling and pulse of a hip tap dancer. His sound was clean and perfect. I haven't heard too many guys play with the kind of depth and technique that Spence had. He could really make that little band move. He was great."

Spencer left the Kirby sextet in 1941 to work briefly with Louis Armstrong, but returned in '42. His career, however, was cut short when, in 1943, he contracted tuberculosis and passed away the very next year at the age of 35.

"I learned about playing brushes from O'Neil Spencer."
—Buddy Rich

Barrett Deems

Directly across the street from the Sherman Hotel in Chicago's Loop, immediately after World War II, stood Randolph Square, billing itself as "The World's Busiest Nite Life Corner." Directly underneath the sign were the words, "Barrett Deems—World's Fastest Drummer."

Deems was born in Springfield, Illinois in 1913. His first professional job was with famed jazz violinist Joe Venuti, who discovered Deems in Springfield and offered him the job with his band. "I joined him in New York in 1937 and stayed until 1945," says Deems. "Kay Starr was on the band—great singer."

A versatile player firmly rooted in the traditional Chicago style of drumming, Deems achieved national acclaim through his performances with the Louis Armstrong All Stars between 1953 and '61. He recorded and toured with Jack Teagarden and Mugsy Spanier, worked the Chicago area with Bill Reinhardt between 1966 and '70, and performed with Joe Kelly's Gaslight Band. Deems also recorded with Art Hodes and made periodic appearances with The World's Greatest Jazz Band. For years he traveled the globe, appearing at many of the world's major all-star jazz festivals. In 1976, Deems toured Europe with Benny Goodman and continues to appear in Europe nearly every year. Early in '86 he spent six weeks touring Europe for the filming of a two-hour video called *The Wonderful World Of Louis Armstrong*. And during 1986 he appeared with Eddie Miller, Milt Hinton, Art Hodes, and Jimmy McPartland at the Newport Jazz Festival in New York.

Throughout a career that has spanned over five decades, Barrett Deems has been acknowledged as a superb player with a clean, effortless swing and outstanding technical ability in the tradition of Chick Webb, Gene Krupa, and Buddy Rich. Excellent examples of his work with Louis Armstrong can be heard on the Columbia Contemporary Masters Collection, *Louis Armstrong: Chicago Concert* (Col C2 36426).

"The older we get, the better we play. If I live to be 90, I'm determined to be playing."
—Barrett Deems

Gene Krupa

Gene Krupa was perhaps the most famous drummer in all of jazz. A key figure in the Chicago style of the late '20s, Krupa spent endless hours in the informal tuition offered by Chicago's black drummers. "Any idea that I knew anything about skins had to go out the window once I started hitting those southside joints. I had no idea of the wide range of effects you could get from a set of drums," said Krupa.

Krupa was born in Chicago's south side in 1909, and was originally marked for the priesthood. After attending a prep seminary, he quit and began drumming around Chicago, first with the Frivolians and later with Ben Pollack, Joe Kayser, and Leo Shukin. He made his recording debut in 1927 with the McKenzie-Condon Chicagoans. After arriving in New York in 1929 with the Red McKenzie band, he worked in pit orchestras for shows like *Girl Crazy* and *Strike Up The Band*, and spent the early '30s with the commercially successful bands of Russ Columbo, Mal Hallet, and Buddy Rogers.

In 1935, Krupa became a member of the Benny Goodman band that would soon become the hottest big band in the nation. Goodman was quickly labeled the "King Of Swing," and Krupa would make his extremely important contribution to jazz drumming within the framework of Goodman's music. His lengthy, fiery solo on "Sing, Sing, Sing" in 1937 led directly to the acceptance of the jazz drummer as a frequently used solo voice in the band.

Krupa left Goodman in 1938 to venture out on his own with a highly successful band that had many hits, including "Drummin' Man," "Drum Boogie," "Wire Brush Stomp," and "Drummer Boy." He remained a big band leader until 1951, after which he toured as a member of the famed *Jazz At The Philharmonic* troupe. The later years of his career were spent leading trios and quartets up until his death in 1973.

Gene Krupa looms large in the evolution of drumming, as much for his musical contributions as for his popularization of the instrument. In essence, he was singly responsible for bringing the drums out from the *background* and into the center-stage spotlight. Occasionally derided by music critics for his elaborate displays of showmanship, Krupa nonetheless was important for his *musical* contribution to jazz, and his influence extends to this day. Absorbing much from Baby Dodds and Chick Webb, Krupa expanded on Dodds' military style and incorporated Webb's technical prowess, meshing the two into one unique drumming style. A master technician, his steady, relentless time feel could be as flexible as George Wettling's and as dynamic as Dave Tough's.

Krupa's work with Goodman—and with his own band—is alive with enthusiasm, wit, and warmth, and his immeasurable influence can be heard in the work of many who followed. The first drummer in jazz history to attain a position of global renown, Gene Krupa is still revered and respected by drummers the world over.

"Gene played an important role in my success. His contribution to the acceptance of jazz is matched by very few."
—Benny Goodman

"He was the first one that made it possible for guys like me to become popular—to be noticed. We all owe him a great deal of gratitude."
—Buddy Rich

Dave Tough

The inimitable Dave Tough controlled every band in which he worked with near-perfect timekeeping and his own distinct, buoyant style. Very much influenced by Baby Dodds, his primary concerns were musicality, maintaining an unwavering pulsation, and integrating the ensemble performance. His playing was subtle yet inspired, and though he rarely soloed—having little technical ability to speak of—he played with an intensity that only a Buddy Rich could match. At a mere 98 pounds, Tough propelled the Woody Herman band with a fire, energy, and drive that was unequaled. He tuned his drums to definite pitches, employed larger cymbals than had previously been used, and made the ride cymbal the basic instrument of his set.

Born in Oak Park, Illinois, Tough jobbed with Bud Freeman and Eddie Condon in the late '20s, and free-lanced in New York with Red Nichols. In 1936 he joined Tommy Dorsey, later working with bands led by Bunny Berrigan, Joe Marsala, Jack Teagarden, Artie Shaw, Benny Goodman, and Charlie Spivak. However, it was his outstanding playing in Woody Herman's mid-'40s band that drove that ensemble to inspired heights, having a profound effect on other drummers, and earning him the acclaim he so well deserved.

Ed Shaughnessy remembers Dave Tough: "I first heard Davey with Woody's band, and it was a great revelation, because he had such *immense* power. He never brought the drums to the forefront, but preferred to simply build a tremendous foundation. When I got to know him, I realized he did many things that were unusual in those days. For instance, he'd keep a wet rag behind the set and wipe the calf bass head to keep it damp. He was also the first drummer I heard who played the bass drum relatively loose. While most drummers were getting a much boomier sound, Davey got a flat sound and used a wooden beater, claiming it didn't interfere with the bass player as far as tonality was concerned. As a result, he was able to play harder with a flatter sound.

"Davey also had one of the finest ears for cymbals I've ever heard," continues Shaughnessy. "Sometimes he'd reinforce brass figures with a little 15" cymbal, where anyone else would have added bass and snare. He didn't like to interrupt the rhythmic flow, so he colored it with the cymbal only. Dave was probably one of the finest examples of someone who didn't have lightening-fast hands and never wanted to solo, but was still one of the most in-demand drummers in the history of jazz."

Dave Tough died from injuries sustained in a fall in Newark, New Jersey in 1948, at the age of 40.

> "I would tell kids to go out and buy his records. They were a lesson in how to play in bands."
> —Henry Adler

> "Dave was the single most musical drummer I've ever known."
> —Artie Shaw

> "When he was with us, the band was at its best—its very best."
> —Woody Herman

Buddy Rich

Buddy Rich was considered a drumming genius, with an astonishing level of speed, control, and endurance that set a whole new standard of excellence for drummers worldwide. Few could match what he did on a set of drums. His playing—always alive with imagination and humor— was a remarkable blending of natural ability and astounding technical excellence. Few drummers failed to acknowledge his phenomenal speed, dexterity, instinctive musical sensitivity, and powerhouse swinging.

Buddy Rich was born in Brooklyn in 1917, and started out with his parents' vaudeville act at the age of 18 months. At age four he was performing on Broadway, and by the age of six he'd toured Australia as "Traps, The Drum Wonder," becoming one of the world's highest-paid child stars. As the vaudeville era faded, Rich decided to seriously pursue a jazz drumming career. By 1938 he was working with Joe Marsala at New York's Hickory House, and soon with bands led by Bunny Berrigan, Artie Shaw, Benny Carter, and Tommy Dorsey.

Following his discharge from the Marine Corps in 1944, Rich rejoined Dorsey, and then formed the first of several bands he would lead. After the swing era he recorded with Charlie Parker, Lionel Hampton, Art Tatum, and Count Basie. Rich toured with *Jazz At The Philharmonic* during the '50s, spent several years with Harry James in Las Vegas, and worked with Charlie Ventura and Les Brown. He also led several small groups up until 1966, when he once again formed his own big band, which he led until his death in 1987.

Buddy Rich's great sense for sparking a band was marvelled at for years by drummers the world over. Though admitting to learning much from Chick Webb, Jo Jones, and Sid Catlett, Rich incorporated many new concepts into jazz drumming with an intensity that was often overwhelming to observers. Possessing incredible speed and coordination of hands and feet, it was said that Rich only needed to hear an arrangement once to play it perfectly. In regards to complete technical mastery of the instrument, no single drummer came any closer to that achievement than Buddy Rich.

"I was quite clear about what my job was by the time I went with Shaw," said Rich in a late interview with writer Burt Korall. "I knew I had to embellish each arrangement, tie it together, keep the time thing going, and inspire the players to be better. My way was to keep the energy level up and push *hard*. This concept was strictly from Harlem. I learned from black drummers like Chick Webb, Jo Jones, and Sid Catlett. In those days, the only reason you were hired was to keep the band together. It was up to you to swing the band, add impetus, and drive. And it certainly helped if you had a feeling for what the arranger wanted. The function of the drummer was to play for the band. And if you were good enough, you'd be noticed."

"Far and away the greatest drummer who ever lived."
—Ray McKinley

"Another like him is not even a possibility."
—Gene Krupa

"Buddy had something no other drummer had, or will ever have."
—Mel Lewis

"The man was a genius. No one will ever equal him."
—Joe Morello

Kenny "Klook" Clarke

Kenny Clarke emerged from the swing bands of the '30s, but was actually the first important drummer of the bop era. Born in Pittsburgh in 1914, Clarke began his career with Roy Eldridge and around the Midwest with the Jeter-Pillars band. He made his first recordings with Edgar Hayes in 1937, and later worked with Claude Hopkins, Teddy Hill, Louis Armstrong, Ella Fitzgerald, and Benny Carter.

Following his army discharge, Clarke returned to New York to join Dizzy Gillespie's big band, where he made numerous recordings. And it's here where we note the first indications of drumming based on the use of the bass drum for accents, the timekeeping function shifting over to the ride cymbal, and the left hand interacting with the soloist. In essence, Kenny Clarke was freeing the drummer from a strictly metronomic role, allowing him the opportunity for more creative interplay, and forcing the bass player to share more of the timekeeping burden.

Kenny Clarke recalled experimenting with a new style of drumming as early as 1940 at Minton's in New York. It was here where his rhythmic ideas meshed with the thinking of young boppers like Dizzy Gillespie, Charlie Christian, Thelonius Monk, and Charlie Parker.

"By 1940, I had everything I was trying to do together," said Clarke. "Before that, I was always thinking, 'There must be an easier, simpler way to keep the band together.' I thought about it for many years. I was still playing the old way, but once in a while I'd do that cymbal thing: *ding-ding-a-ding*. I figured you could hear the time better than on the snare drum. The bottom never changed. I just put the time up on the cymbal to ease the weight of the bass drum. I'd tell the guys to put the time in their heads and play. Once they got it in their heads, I went upstairs to stay. I played the time up there, and it gave my left hand the freedom to do other things."

Later in his career, Clarke worked on 52nd Street with Tadd Dameron's sextet, where his relaxed style was a modern extension of the feeling Jo Jones had achieved with the Basie band. His playing had become a synthesis of previous approaches, most notably the ride cymbal of Jo Jones, the unpredictable, explosive solos of Sid Catlett, and the timbral variations of Baby Dodds.

Clarke continued to free-lance around New York with important modernists, and in 1952 was instrumental in the formation of the legendary Modern Jazz Quartet. In 1956, he left for Paris, where he took up residence and remained until his death in 1985. More than any player who had come before, Kenny Clarke gave jazz drummers an opportunity to fully express themselves, unleashing the chains that had bound them up to that point. His unique concepts would eventually impact on every jazz drummer the world over.

"Klook played drums the way I would have played if I played drums."
—Dizzy Gillespie

"I didn't like the way other drummers were playing. I wanted to be able to say, 'Look, this is the way I play.'"
—Kenny Clarke

—41

Max Roach

Max Roach was perhaps the most important drummer to come out of the '40s. With a style influenced by Sid Catlett, Jo Jones, and Kenny Clarke, Roach took the basic conceptual tools and fashioned his own way of playing. Where Clarke was the ground-breaker, Roach elaborated on the new style with greater complexity, becoming the perfect accompanist for modernists like Bud Powell, Dizzy Gillespie, and Charlie Parker. Max Roach literally set the standards for the bop drummer of the '40s.

Roach was born in North Carolina in 1925, grew up in Brooklyn, and took up drums at the age of 10. "Jo Jones was the first drummer I heard who played broken rhythms," said Roach. "I listened to him over and over again. But a lot of people inspired me. Chick Webb was a tremendous soloist. There was Sonny Greer, Cozy Cole, and Sid Catlett, who incorporated this hi-hat and ride cymbal style. Then I heard Kenny. He exemplified personality and did more with the instrument. It meant more. *It affected me.*"

After graduating from Boys High, Roach worked at Kelly's Stables with Coleman Hawkins, and was then hired by Dizzy Gillespie to play at New York's Onyx Club in '44. He later worked with Benny Carter, the Parker-Gillespie quintet, and then with Parker and Miles Davis. In 1947, Roach became Charlie Parker's regular drummer. "Bird's approach demanded new drumming concepts," said Roach. "He set tempos so fast it was impossible to play a straight four, so we had to work out new variations."

It was Roach's playing on the Savoy and Dial recordings made between 1947 and '49 that would make him the most widely imitated and influential drummer of his time. His use of the ride cymbal to establish a more *legato* feel was emulated by countless drummers. And a Roach solo was a giant step towards a more melodic approach to drumming. Where Sid Catlett had thought in terms of two-bar phrases, Roach expanded it to *four*, which gave his solos a strong internal balance and melodiousness. Many of Roach's solos are considered masterpieces of melodic and rhythmic inventiveness contoured in a most imaginative manner.

According to Roach, "When I build a solo, it's a design within the structure of something, like creating a poem or a painting. Space and dynamics are important, and things like sequences. How you relate to certain timbres on the set itself is important. That's how you build a solo."

During the mid-'50s, Roach toured with *Jazz At The Philharmonic*, and then teamed with trumpeter Clifford Brown and pianist Richie Powell to form one of the most exciting jazz groups in history. Since then he's led a host of highly successful small groups, taught at the University of Massachusetts, and spearheaded M'Boom, a contemporary percussion ensemble made up of jazz drummers.

Max Roach has been credited with breaking down more barriers than any other drummer in the history of jazz. He was one of the first artists to record in odd time signatures, to solo with bass accompaniment, and even utilize timpani in a jazz context. The body of work produced by Max Roach is virtually unmatched, and he has deservedly earned his place among the all-time greats of modern drumming.

"I really tuned into Max for solos."
—Louis Hayes

"Max has always been a fabulous musician."
—Philly Joe Jones.

"He showed us what had to be done. He changed the course of drumming."
—Stan Levey

Tiny Kahn

The bop era of the '40s saw the arrival of several somewhat lesser-known drummers. One of the most important was Tiny Kahn. "Tiny and I were both advocates of the small group approach to big band playing," said Mel Lewis. "He played basically the same with Stan Getz's small group as he did with Chubby Jackson's big band. Tiny had the flexibility to complement whoever he was playing with. He had a light bass drum attack, used the whole spectrum of the drumset, and played with simplicity amidst this constant subtle motion."

Tiny Kahn was born in New York in 1924 and began playing at age 15. Possessing a highly stylized approach—which he'd subtly adjust for different bands—Kahn played with Georgie Auld, Boyd Raeburn, Henry Jerome, and was a key figure in the 1949 Chubby Jackson band. He later worked with Charlie Barnet, and Stan Getz, and did a CBS radio show with Elliot Lawrence. Kahn was also a proficient vibist, arranger, and composer who contributed arrangements to the music libraries of the Chubby Jackson, Charlie Barnet, and Woody Herman bands.

Though somewhat underrated throughout his brief career, Kahn was among the most capable of jazz drummers, with a knack for making his bandmates totally comfortable. Though he had little technical flair and rarely engaged in displays of showmanship, Kahn was renowned for his superb timekeeping and melodic playing, the latter an obvious result of his arranging and composing background. Like Jo Jones, Kahn displayed an extraordinary sense of shading and dynamics. Never one to overplay, his soft pulse and loose feel—combined with perfectly placed fills—were tailored to the music, making him one of the most distinctive players of his time.

"Tiny brought the improvisational feeling of small band drumming to the big band," said Mel Lewis. "He played great fills and lead-ins that kicked the band along. He knew how to use space and never played too loud. Tiny was a straightforward player with a certain looseness, and his own kind of chops. His style was truly a combination of Davey Tough and a more simplified Max Roach. The man was an extremely musical player—a real listening drummer. His way of playing just worked." Tiny Kahn died in 1953 at the age of 29.

"He did what was necessary and knocked everybody out."
—Terry Gibbs

"The most musical drummer I ever encountered."
—Red Rodney

"One of my favorite drummers of all time."
—Stan Getz

Shadow Wilson

Though not a major influence in the same sense as Max Roach and Kenny Clarke, Shadow Wilson was nonetheless in considerable demand during the '40s, and he fit in admirably with all the groups he played with during his relatively brief career.

Wilson was born in Yonkers, New York in 1919 and began his career with Frank Fairfax. By 1939, he was working in bands led by Lucky Millinder and Jimmy Mundy. In 1940, he performed with Benny Carter and Tiny Bradshaw, and then moved on to the Earl Hines band. However, Wilson is best remembered for his tasteful work with the Count Basie band, with whom he played in 1944. Wilson spent two years with tenor saxophonist Illinois Jacquet, won the prestigious *Esquire* New Star Award in 1947, and then returned to the Basie band as a replacement for Papa Jo Jones.

According to jazz legend, upon Dave Tough's departure from the Woody Herman band in '48, the musicians took a vote to determine who would replace Tough. Shadow Wilson was elected, however, pleased with the Basie band, he refused the offer. Members of Herman's band did eventually get their wish when Wilson joined up in '49, once again proving his ability as a superb big band drummer as well as a highly competent small group player.

After leaving Herman, Wilson returned to Illinois Jacquet's group in 1950 and again in '54, with the years between spent with young piano sensation Erroll Garner. Late in his career Wilson worked with Ella Fitzgerald, and was also acclaimed for his performances with Thelonius Monk in the '50s.

Though Shadow Wilson died in 1959 at the age of 40, numerous examples of his recorded performances have been preserved. Among those recordings are "Queer Street" with the Basie Band, *Jacquet Jumps*, *The Fabulous Fats Navarro* with Tadd Dameron, and assorted recordings with Lester Young, Leo Parker, and Stan Getz. Every Wilson performance clearly demonstrates the tasteful, unobtrusive playing of one of the jazz world's true unsung heroes.

"Like a young Jo Jones, Shadow had superb taste. I had great respect for him."
—Don Lamond

"He could swing you into bad health."
—Kenny Washington

Roy Haynes

Of the many drummers to come out of the Max Roach school, Roy Haynes was perhaps the most prolific. Influenced by Clarke and Roach, Haynes has been called a latter-day Jo Jones with respect to his superb taste and versatility, which made him effective over a wide spectrum of jazz styles with a wide range of players.

Haynes was born in Roxbury, Massachusetts in 1926, and started out playing in Boston as a teenager with Phil Edmunds and Sabby Lewis. He came to New York in 1945 to work with Luis Russell at Harlem's Savoy Ballroom, and two years later joined Lester Young. By '49, Haynes was playing on 52nd Street with people like Kai Winding, Stan Getz, and legendary alto saxophonist Charlie Parker.

Haynes recalled the Parker association: "If there ever was one genius in my career, it was Charlie Parker. It was a thrill just to *be* there, to be on the bandstand. The drums seemed to play themselves when I was with him. Playing with Bird was like being born again. Each time we'd play the music was more elevated. I didn't do anything different technically; I was just trying to learn more. I would listen—just grasp."

In the early '50s Haynes worked with jazz vocalists Billie Holiday and Ella Fitzgerald, and in '53 he became Sarah Vaughan's regular drummer. During the '60s he performed with a variety of name players including Gary Burton, Phineas Newborn, Miles Davis, Lee Konitz, Eric Dolphy, and Kenny Burrell, and as a sub for Elvin Jones with jazz great John Coltrane. "Coltrane gave me complete freedom of expression," said Haynes. "He understood a lot of the things I was trying to do. It really felt like we were on the same wavelength."

Writer Jeff Potter offers an accurate perspective of Roy Haynes: "It's often said that Roy and Elvin were the drummers most responsible for challenging the tyranny of the 2 and 4 hi-hat. The end of dependence on the 2 and 4 was compounded by increasingly asymmetric syncopations, as drummers and bass players implied bar lines more than defined them. But the truth is, Roy's feel and musical concept *always* tended towards this direction. The rhythmic elasticity heard from groups like Coltrane's quartet merely brought to the public's attention what Roy had on the burner for years. Roy didn't change to better-fit '60s jazz; '60s jazz changed and better fit Roy."

Haynes has gone on to perform with other name artists including Pat Metheny and Chick Corea, along with leading his own popular Hip Ensemble. With an illustrious career that has spanned over five decades, Roy Haynes takes his place among the all-time greats.

"Roy is the easiest drummer to play with, yet he's also the most interesting."
—Pat Metheny

"One of the best drummers I've worked with."
—John Coltrane

"Roy's style is so unique that no other drummer has ever really copied it."
—Jack DeJohnette

Stan Levey

A graduate of the Max Roach school, and an influential player in his own right, Stan Levey was a key figure in the development of the techniques that further modernized jazz drumming. "Bird and Max were responsible for the way I thought about music," claimed Levey. "I came to realize that being musical was the most important thing. Just sit down and do the job. Play time and make the other players feel good."

Levey was born in Philadelphia in 1925, began playing at the age of 7, and studied piano and arranging in high school. His career began around the Philadelphia area, where he played with Dizzy Gillespie. After his arrival in New York in '44, he worked with bassist Oscar Pettiford, and again with Gillespie at New York's famed Onyx. An accepted member of the New York jazz fraternity, Levey was a popular figure on 52nd Street, working with artists such as Allen Eager, Coleman Hawkins, Ben Webster, Erroll Garner, Thelonius Monk, Barney Bigard, and George Shearing.

By 1945, he was working on the Street with bop pioneers Dizzy Gillespie and Charlie Parker, and clearly recalls the experience: "They were out of this world. Playing with them was the pinnacle. There might have been pressure because the musicians were so good and you had to produce. But the love for the music was so great that you didn't feel the pressure."

Though initially influenced by Chick Webb, Levey remembers hearing Max Roach for the first time. "It was like lightening had struck me. I never heard time split up like that. The approach was different than anything I had come across. A drummer now had to color and give the music a more well-rounded feeling. He had to be a *contributor*."

Equally at home in big bands and small groups, Levey also worked with Georgie Auld, Freddie Slack, Stan Kenton, and Charlie Ventura, and in 1945 subbed for Dave Tough in Woody Herman's band. Following a few years of partial inactivity, he returned to the Stan Kenton band in '52. "It was a tough, physically demanding job," says Levey. "I almost had to start working with weights to keep up with it—probably the band was too overpowering. You couldn't move or maneuver the thing too easily."

Happier in the small group environment, Levey later joined Howard Rumsey's Lighthouse Allstars in California, where he remained for six years. After touring with vocalists Peggy Lee and Ella Fitzgerald, he became part of the prestigious L.A. studio scene and recorded with everyone from Henry Mancini to Frank Sinatra.

A capable, innovative player who made a meaningful contribution to bop drumming, Stan Levey retired in 1972 to pursue a lifelong interest in photography.

"Stan was the first white drummer who could really play modern jazz."
—Phil Brown

"...a forceful, energetic, excellent player."
—Irv Kluger

Don Lamond

Don Lamond, considered one of the finest big band drummers to achieve prominence during the mid-'40s, was born in Oklahoma City in 1920 and raised in Washington, D.C. His interest in drums began in grade school, and by high school he had already formed his own band. Following his studies with Horace Butterworth and at the Peabody Institute in Baltimore, Lamond landed his first name band job with Sonny Dunham in 1943. In '45, after a year with Boyd Raeburn's band, he was called to replace Dave Tough in the Woody Herman band, where he remained until the band's breakup. When Herman reformed as the famed "Four Brothers" band in 1947, Lamond was called back and soon achieved his well-deserved recognition.

"I was lucky to be coming up at a time when the great black drummers were around," said Lamond. "Sid Catlett, Jo Jones, Jimmy Crawford, and Cozy Cole—they were good to me. I met them all when I was with Woody. I didn't even know Gene or Buddy at the time. Sid was my favorite. Max was around then, too. He was 19 when I met him."

Regarding Woody Herman, Lamond remembers him as a great guy to work for. "He always had young guys in the band. He let you get away with murder, but you *knew* he was the boss. He always made you play your best."

Known for his great drum sound, reminiscent of Dave Tough, Lamond recalls, "I never had a hard bass drum sound. I was influenced by Davey. He tuned his drums differently from anyone I'd ever heard. The sound of his cymbals and the tension of his bass drum were unique, and I realized how well soft drums blended with the band. I'd get the heads at the same tension, and then back off a little on the batter side. I also used newspaper inside the bass drum."

After Herman disbanded in '49, Lamond remained in Los Angeles for a brief period, and then moved to New York, where he became busy on record dates and on the Steve Allen, Perry Como, Pat Boone, and Garry Moore TV shows. In 1972, he left the New York studio scene to settle in Florida, first to front his own big band, and then to co-lead a band at Disney World in Orlando.

Of all the new players to emerge on the music scene during the '40s, Don Lamond was a key force in carrying forward the big band drumming tradition previously carved out by Sid Catlett, Jo Jones, and Dave Tough.

> "I was raised to believe in swinging the band—not in soloing."
> —Don Lamond

Shelly Manne

A direct offshoot of bop, the west coast "cool" school proved to be a more subdued, relaxed form of jazz that incorporated stylized arrangements, classically influenced harmonies, exotic flavorings and instrumentations, and brilliant tone colors. Gathering momentum in the early '50s, west coast drumming was marked by the complexity of odd groupings and the hint of unusual tonalities. Pushing back tonal barriers with his expert use of sticks, brushes, mallets, hands, fingers, tambourines, triangles, and even silver dollars rolled on tom-toms, Shelly Manne is recognized as the essential founder of the school.

Manne was born in New York in 1920 and studied with Billy Gladstone. Following his first professional job on an ocean liner to Europe, he worked with bands led by Bobby Byrne, Benny Goodman, Joe Marsala, Raymond Scott, Will Bradley, and Les Brown. Stationed in Brooklyn during the war years, Manne stayed in close touch with the developments on 52nd Street through 1945. According to Manne, "The most important lesson I learned on 52nd Street was that you better swing your ass off or you weren't going to be around too long."

After a stint with Stan Kenton's band, Manne toured with *Jazz At The Philharmonic* in '49, worked with Woody Herman that same year, and then rejoined Kenton in 1950. Settling in California in '52, he played with Howard Rumsey and Shorty Rogers, and then became one of the most successful drummers on the L.A. studio scene.

Despite his prominence in the studios, Manne never lost his jazz roots, performing on more than half of the hundreds of jazz recordings to come out of Los Angeles. Winner of the *down beat* and *Metronome* polls year after year, he firmly established himself as one of the most tasteful, swinging, and inventive drummers of his time. Always the colorist, Manne made wide use of tonal effects and showed great concern for melodic drumming. Known for tuning his drums to definite pitches—which enabled him to play melodies in the *true* sense of the word—Manne was a solid swinger and one of the most technically proficient drummers in jazz.

"Instead of letting the rhythm imply its own melody, my concept is to play melodically and allow the melody to create rhythm," said Manne. "My ideas are linearly conceived and executed, often in opposition to the structure of the bar lines. Improvisation is the result of *melodic*, not rhythmic thinking."

Despite his active studio schedule, Manne was considered to be among one of the most dynamic voices in modern jazz. Shelly Manne passed away in 1984.

"The most beautiful concept drummer you'd ever want to hear."
—Jim Keltner

"Shelly didn't play drums. Shelly played music."
—Emil Richards

"One of the most musical drummers I've ever heard."
—Joe Morello

Chico Hamilton

Following closely in the tradition of Shelly Manne and Max Roach, in terms of tonal experimentation and melodic thinking, was Chico Hamilton, born in Los Angeles in 1921. "If I had to describe my way of playing, I would say that I caress the instrument as opposed to hitting it," said Hamilton during a 1985 *MD* interview. "I guess that's the difference. I couldn't care less about being the world's fastest, or whatever. I'm more interested in achieving a sound out of the instrument."

Hamilton was influenced early on by Sonny Greer, and performed with the Duke Ellington band at the age of 16. He began his professional career with Lionel Hampton and Lester Young, and later toured with Count Basie and Jimmy Mundy. A student of Papa Jo Jones during his Army tenure, Hamilton built a solid reputation as a sensitive player. His distinctive style and graceful touch made him popular among vocalists like Ella Fitzgerald, Billie Holiday, Tony Bennett, Billy Eckstine, and Nat King Cole. In 1948, he began working with singer Lena Horne, an association that would endure off and on for the next eight years.

"Every singer in the world sings with the drummer," recalled Hamilton. "The bass drum plays a very important part in the way they phrase. And playing as an accompanist for Lena called for every ounce of musicianship I had."

In 1952 Hamilton became a founding member of the Gerry Mulligan quartet, and in the mid-'50s he formed his own quintet featuring guitar, cello, reeds, bass, and drums. Often referred to as "chamber jazz," the group's unorthodox instrumentation was the perfect setting for Hamilton's unique textural approach. Delicate mallet playing on perfectly pitched tom-toms and impeccable brush work combined to make his refined concept one of the highlights of mid-'50s jazz drumming.

Later in his career, Hamilton worked as a staff player at Paramount Studios and became proficient at scoring. A move back east followed, along with the formation of Chico Hamilton Productions, a successful company for the production of music for radio, TV, and films.

Hamilton has also been credited with being among the first to use a 16" bass drum, and one of the first—if not *the* first—to use single-headed toms to control pitch. With a concept firmly rooted in the *natural* sound of drums, Chico Hamilton's artistic approach reflected a classic refinement of jazz drumming, and a musical spirit open to new forms of percussive expression.

> "It's not the melodic aspect of music that's the universal language—it's the rhythm. It's the pulsation."
> —Chico Hamilton

Louie Bellson

ouie Bellson, born in Rock Fall, Illinois in 1924, studied drums with Bert Winans and Roy Knapp, and won the Gene Krupa Drum Contest as a teenager. His first professional job was with the Ted Fio Rito band, which he joined at 17. After leaving Fio Rito, Bellson was hired by Benny Goodman as a replacement for Gene Krupa, an experience he fondly recalls: "Benny taught me how to really work in a rhythm section," remembers Bellson, "to be aware of the band and play for the band. When it's time to play a solo, then it's your time to shine, but until *then* you're an accompanist. And the most important thing is to make that band swing. Solos are secondary. If you're a great soloist but can't swing the band, forget it."

Bellson spent 1947-'50 with the Tommy Dorsey band, and then went on to play with Harry James. After leaving James, he moved into the driver's seat of the Duke Ellington band, where he remained until 1953. Credited with revitalizing the Ellington band during his two-year stay, Bellson also contributed arrangements, most notably "Hawk Talks" and "Skin Deep," a legendary drumming tour de force.

An extraordinary technician with an explosive and dynamic solo style, Bellson is noted for his razor-sharp timing and aggressive propulsion of the many big bands and small groups he's performed with over the years. He is also recognized as the first drummer to successfully utilize double bass drums. Though he conceived the idea in 1938, it wasn't until 1946—after his return to the Ted Fio Rito band—that he actually began to utilize it.

"I had a certain amount of agility and ambidexterity," recalls Bellson, "and I sat down one day and thought, 'How would it be to have another bass drum over there and still utilize the hi-hat?' I took it to various drum companies, and they thought I was crazy. They weren't really saying, 'Get out of here, kid.' But they *were* saying, 'Are you sure you want something like that, because that's not really what guys are doing.'"

During the mid-'50s, Bellson worked with the Tommy and Jimmy Dorsey Orchestra, and in later years toured with his wife, Pearl Bailey. Along with being an author, composer, and clinician, Bellson has also continued to front his own big band in an effort to keep the tradition of big band jazz alive. For more than five decades, Louie Bellson's enthusiasm, drive, technique, and dedication to the art of drumming have made him one of the jazz world's most influential and highly-regarded drummers.

"The world's greatest drummer—Bellson has all the requirements for perfection in his craft."
—Duke Ellington

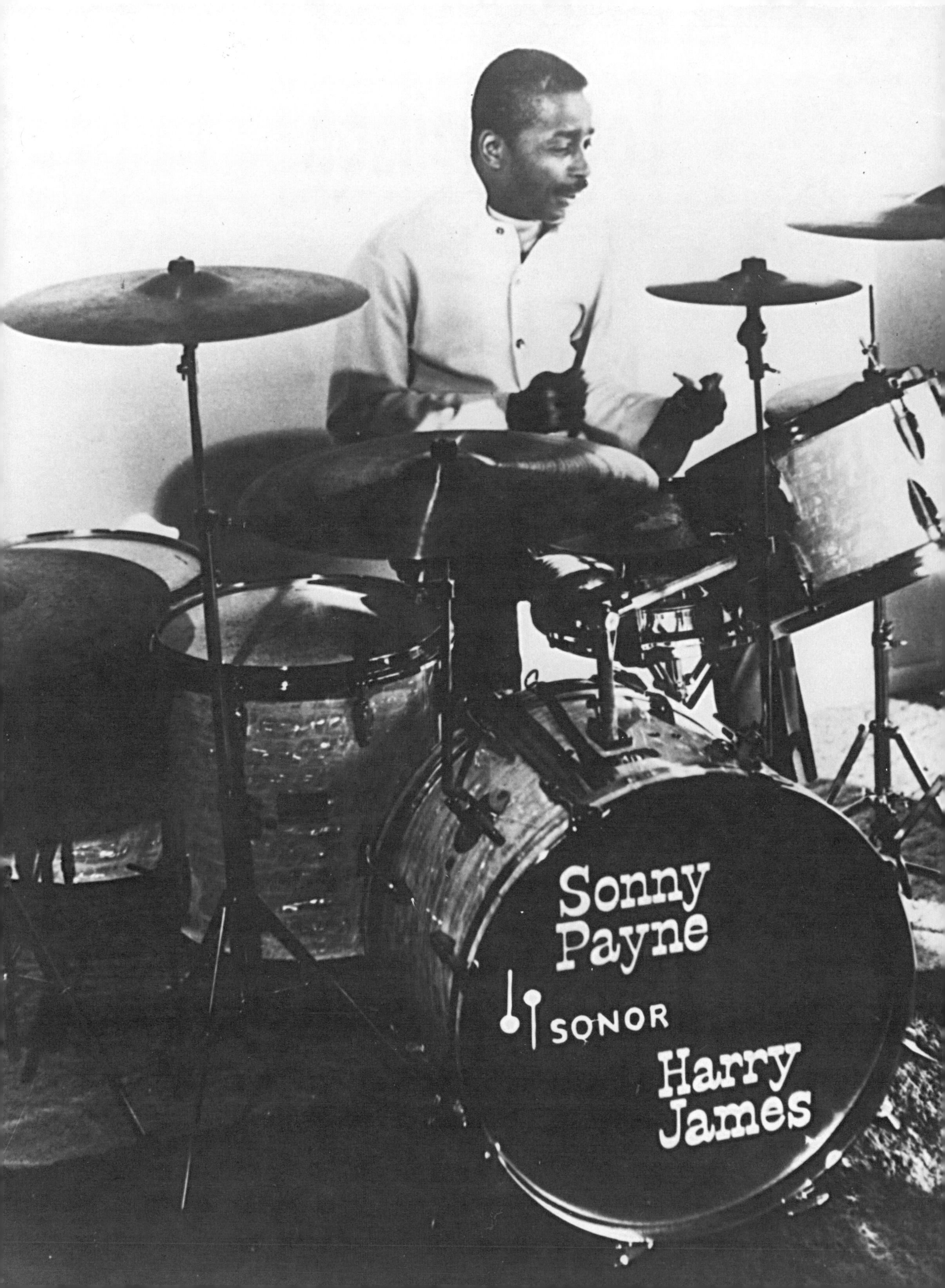
Sonny
Payne
SONOR
Harry
James

Sonny Payne

By the mid-'50s, most of the major big bands that had so strongly dominated the music scene during the prior two decades had all but disappeared. The majority of bands had either broken up completely, or were now condensed down to smaller combos. However, there were a few exceptions to the trend, one of which was the Count Basie band. After Papa Jo Jones left in '48, Basie had been through several drummers. And though all were competent players, no one really seemed to adequately fill the great void left by Jones—that is until the arrival of Sonny Payne in 1955.

Payne was born in New York in 1926. He played with Tiny Grimes, Lucille Dixon, Earl Bostic, Hot Lips Page, and the Erskine Hawkins Orchestra, led his own trio and quintet, and worked with Frank Sinatra after leaving Basie. Payne also had a long tenure with trumpeter Harry James, but returned to the Basie band, where he remained until 1974. The later years of his life were spent touring with Don Cunningham and Company.

During his key years with Basie (1955-'65), Payne displayed a flamboyant style very much in the tradition of Chick Webb and Gene Krupa. Accused by some music critics of going overboard in terms of flash—which could occasionally detract from the subtlety of the Basie band—Payne nonetheless injected the band with a lively musical spirit that had been missing since the departure of Jones seven years earlier. According to some jazz historians, Payne was perhaps the most *exciting* drummer to ever sit in the driver's seat of the Basie band.

Butch Miles, who played with Basie during the late '70s, remembered Sonny Payne: "Sonny was one of the greatest big band drummers I ever saw. He played with fire, enthusiasm, and intelligence."

Along with his infectious drive and color, Payne was also known for his thunderous fills, abrupt pauses, exaggerated technical flourishes, and dramatic shifts in dynamics. Payne drove the Basie band with an intensity matched by few other big band drummers. Throughout its existence, the Basie band maintained a relaxed ensemble precision few bands could emulate, and a distinct rhythm section feel that, years earlier, had established it as one of the best in jazz. Sonny Payne's ability to maintain the character of the band, while incorporating aspects of his own dynamic personality into this established framework, is undeniable. Sonny Payne passed away in 1979.

> "When Sonny was right, I don't think I've ever heard another drummer sound so good."
> —Butch Miles

Art Blakey

"Art Blakey brought a new kind of primal force and simplicity to jazz drumming," said writer Chip Stern in an *MD* interview. "Anchored by a persistent 2-4 hi-hat pulse and hissing K Zildjian cymbals, Blakey streamlined the swinging groove of bebop, making it less busy and spasmodic. At the same time, he managed to synthesize the tonal approach of West African drummers with the grit of American blues."

Blakey was born in Pittsburgh in 1919. He began as a pianist, but switched to drums after hearing Erroll Garner. He clearly recalled the early years of his lengthy career: "I used to play every night. We'd get through at 6:00 A.M. Then we'd play the breakfast show. After that we'd have a jam session until 2:00 in the afternoon. Maybe by 3:00 I'd get to bed, but I'd be back in the club again at 8:30. I didn't have to worry about practicing. I was playing all the time."

Blakey's first break came in 1939, when he joined the Fletcher Henderson band. After leaving Henderson and working with Marylou Williams in the early '40s, Blakey played in the legendary Billy Eckstine band from 1944 to 1947, with artists like Dexter Gordon, Dizzy Gillespie, Charlie Parker, Fats Navarro, Miles Davis, and Sarah Vaughan. "The idea of that band was to play like a small combo," said Blakey. "They didn't read music. They gave you two or three weeks to learn the book, and if you didn't commit it to memory, you were *fired*. You followed the first alto, and whatever he did you had better follow. Wherever the first trumpet led, you followed. Wherever the first trombone led, you followed."

In 1955, Blakey formed the first of his Jazz Messengers groups, which he continued to lead up until his death in 1990. For 35 years, Blakey's Messengers set the standard for small-group hard bop, and were launching pads for great young players like Kenny Dorham, Lee Morgan, Bobby Timmons, Wayne Shorter, Curtis Fuller, Horace Silver, and Wynton Marsalis.

One of the most recorded drummers in jazz history, Blakey possessed an explosive, hard-swinging style, heavily injected with West African flavor. Known for his powerful drive and rock-steady time, Blakey made his mark as one of the great ensemble burners of all time. Heavy accentuation of 2 and 4 in the ride pattern, and a biting hi-hat that stayed on the very front edge of the beat, gave Blakey's drumming a fire that few could match. Polyrhythmic rim clicks behind soloists, the roar of a press roll *crescendo* between phrases, and strong Afro-Cuban influences were more of Blakey's contributions to the jazz drummer's vocabulary. Though many attempted to copy his style, Art Blakey was an original in the true sense of the word, with few (if any) equals in the hard bop idiom.

"He taught me how to build a solo to a climax."
—Bobby Timmons

"Art had an ability to spot talent. But once he spotted it, he cultivated it."
—Horace Silver

"The swing man—always hard driving and in control of the music."
—Jack DeJohnette

Philly Joe Jones

Philly Joe Jones is considered by many to be one of the most important drummers in jazz. His emotionally charged playing was the perfect combination of Sid Catlett's subtlety, Art Blakey's fire, and the melodiousness of Max Roach.

Jones was born in Philadelphia in 1923, and after working with local bands, moved to New York, where he played with Joe Morris, Tiny Grimes, and Arnette Cobb. By the early '50s, he was in great demand for recording sessions with people like Lou Donaldson, Clifford Brown, Lee Morgan, and Freddie Hubbard, and as house drummer at Prestige Records.

After studying with Cozy Cole, Jones' growing versatility enabled him to handle work with big bands led by Duke Ellington, Tadd Dameron, and later, with Buddy Rich. However, it wasn't until 1954—as an integral member of the Miles Davis band featuring Davis, John Coltrane, Red Garland, and Paul Chambers—that Jones would be revered by jazz fans and drummers alike. Between 1954 and '58, his solid drive, masterful brushwork, and melodically inventive solos influenced an entire generation of drummers.

Jones recalled the Davis years: "It was my greatest experience in the music business," he said. "I don't think I'll *ever* be associated with four people like Miles, 'Trane, Red, and Paul again. That was like a factory. We were all learning from each other. Miles was really the teacher. Everything he would say was valuable. Now when I look back, I realize how much I learned from him about rhythm and time, and how to play around with the time and still make it right. That was a total experience. I must have left Miles two or three times, but then I'd think about it, and I'd go back."

After the Davis years, Jones toured with Bill Evans and Dizzy Gillespie, and free-lanced extensively on both coasts. During the '70s he moved to Europe, where he performed with his own group, gigged with Slide Hampton and Dizzy Reece, and taught at Kenny Clarke's drum school in Paris. Along with performing, teaching became an important part of Jones' life on his return to the States, and up until his passing in 1985.

Strongly rooted in the style of Blakey and Roach, Jones goes down in jazz history as one of the greatest of the hard boppers. In retrospect, Philly Joe Jones would prove to be the *strongest* link in the chain between Roach, Haynes, and Blakey, and the Elvin Jones/Tony Williams school soon to emerge.

"Philly Joe played some stuff that knocked me out."
—Omar Hakim

"I really liked the way he took rudiments and made them swing."
—Jack DeJohnette

Jimmy Cobb

Jimmy Cobb was one of the most popular players of the late '50s. He began playing at an early age and found his influences among the bop pioneers. "Max Roach was the hippest music going," remembers Cobb. "I also listened to Kenny Clarke, Shadow Wilson, and Sid Catlett. Then a little later there was Art Blakey and Philly Joe Jones."

Cobb was born in Washington, D.C. in 1929, began his professional career with Billie Holiday, and later worked with tenor saxophonist Charlie Rouse. After moving to New York at 21, Cobb played with Earl Bostic's band for a year, and then went on to work with Dinah Washington, Cannonball Adderley, Dizzy Gillespie, and Stan Getz.

In 1958, after building a strong reputation as an adaptable jazz drummer, Cobb became a key member of the Miles Davis group featuring Cannonball Adderley and John Coltrane. This line-up can be heard on Davis' *Kind Of Blue* album, where Cobb's spirited time feel contributes to the success of this classic recording.

One of the most solid time players to ever grace the jazz scene, Cobb spoke on the subject in a 1979 *MD* interview: "I think the best way to improve your time is to play with musicians who *have* good time. You've got to listen to guys that play good time and get a feeling for it. Then you can go home and practice it. You can hear that feeling."

A highly imaginative player, Cobb also performed with Miles Davis and Gil Evans on the *Porgy And Bess* and *Sketches Of Spain* LPs. After leaving Davis in '62, he teamed with bassist Paul Chambers and pianist Wynton Kelly to form a trio that at one point backed up famed guitarist Wes Montgomery. When Montgomery left to form his own group, Kelly, Cobb, and Chambers stayed together until Chambers' death in '69. Cobb and Kelly remained together until Cobb joined jazz vocalist Sarah Vaughan in 1971.

Still actively free-lancing with leading jazz players, Jimmy Cobb is admired by jazz fans and drummers alike.

"Jimmy has everything I like in a drummer."
—Stan Levey

Louis Hayes

Louis Hayes was rooted in the romping, hard bop tradition of Philly Joe Jones. His drumming career began in the Detroit area, where he was born, though he later worked with a host of different bands in the south. Hayes recalled his early influences during a mid-'80s *MD* interview: "I listened to Kenny Clarke really well. I mean I listened my buns off. I was paying attention. And that's how I developed my cymbal beat. I also heard Max on records, and I really liked his mind. He has a very intelligent mind on the drums. Those two people were my basic influences."

Hayes' career began to take root in 1955 after joining Yusef Lateef's group, a setting that brought him to the attention of jazz pianist Horace Silver. After joining Silver in '56, the band quickly established itself as one of the seminal jazz groups of the hard bop movement, later known as "soul jazz." By 1959, perhaps the hottest jazz group in the country was the Cannonball Adderley Quintet, and Hayes was the perfect choice for the drum spot, which he held steadily for seven years. Being there from the onset of both the Silver and Adderley bands, Hayes had an opportunity to literally *set* the drum sound for both leaders.

"I had total freedom with those groups," said Hayes. "During all my years with Horace and Cannon, there was never anything like reading music for me. It was, 'Louis, this is the way it goes. Now put it together because you can put it together better than I can. Play what you want to play.' They just gave me the format, and I did the rest."

In 1965, Hayes replaced Ed Thigpen in Oscar Peterson's trio, and continued on and off with Peterson for the next five years. A stint with Freddie Hubbard filled the next several years, prior to his rejoining Peterson for another year. In '72, Hayes organized his own quintet, which later featured Woody Shaw and Dexter Gordon. By 1975, he was coleading a quintet with Junior Cook, which toured throughout Europe. Hayes has continued to front his own groups, and to perform with other prominent jazz artists over the years.

Popular with many leading players, Hayes has recorded with John Coltrane, J.J. Johnson, Phineas Newborn, Wes Montgomery, Lee Morgan, Sonny Stitt, and Cedar Walton, among others. A dynamic yet sensitive drummer in the classic hard bop tradition, Louis Hayes carried forward what Art Blakey and Philly Joe Jones had started, with an infectious "on top of the beat" feel that never lacked in energy and enthusiasm.

"We rehearsed plenty. We weren't just playing around. We sat down, put it together, and rehearsed."
—Louis Hayes

Alan Dawson

In 1957, Alan Dawson began teaching at the Berklee School of Music, and over the next 18 years produced students the caliber of Keith Copeland, Steve Smith, Kenwood Dennard, Harvey Mason, John Robinson, Vinnie Colaiuta, and Tony Williams.

"I never set out to be a teacher," said Dawson in an *MD* interview. "I became a teacher because people expressed an interest in what I was doing. I like to think I teach music, and the drum happens to be one of the instruments with which to create and communicate musical ideas. In teaching someone, I want that person first to be a *musician*. The pupil must have an understanding, appreciation, and respect for the music itself."

Dawson was born in Marietta, Pennsylvania in 1929 and began playing locally in 1943. He was strongly influenced by Papa Jo Jones, and his first break came in the early '50s with the Lionel Hampton band. By 1951 he was working with Sabby Lewis and building a solid reputation as a superb jazz drummer in the Boston area.

Dawson was known for his ingenious use of rudiments, his melodic approach to drumming, and an extremely advanced level of hand and foot coordination. He elaborated on some of his insightful concepts: "Coordination is a nice thing to have going. But taken to extremes, you set up rhythmic interference instead of maintaining a groove. It becomes a case of having things running so counter to each other that the whole thing stops swinging. And when we speak of melodic drumming, we aren't actually playing melody, per se. We're making people *hear* melodies by dealing with approximations of pitch, and by the combination of rhythms that go with certain melodies. When you're thinking melody, it becomes obvious because the phrases wind up being more fluid."

Between 1963 and 1970, Dawson was house drummer at Lennie's in Boston, where he backed the numerous artists who passed through. "Some people would get hold of the records of someone they knew they were going to play with," said Dawson. "I never did cram for those jobs. I would think about the things I had heard these people play, rather than about what their *drummers* had done."

A resourceful soloist with rock steady time, Dawson spent 1968 through 1974 with the Dave Brubeck Quartet featuring Gerry Mulligan and Jack Six. Although revered as an astute teacher, Alan Dawson's popularity among musicians resulted from his being one of the most tasteful, meticulous, and intelligent players on the jazz scene. His performances with artists like Phil Woods, Jaki Byard, Richard Davis, Booker Ervin, Al Cohn, Reggie Workman, Oscar Peterson, Sonny Stitt, Dexter Gordon, Phineas Newborn, Quincy Jones, George Shearing, Tal Farlow, Earl Hines, and Hank Jones certainly substantiate that fact.

"I consider him to be a key man. We trembled when we knew we had to deal with him."
—Max Roach

Connie Kay

While the hard-driving, straight-ahead drumming of Jones, Blakey, Cobb, and Hayes supplied the undercurrent for the majority of small groups during the '50s and '60s, Connie Kay saw fit to break the mold with his own unique brand of subtle, musical drumming. Kay was born in Tuckahoe, New York in 1927. Early notoriety came when he worked with Charles Thompson and Miles Davis at Minton's in New York during the early days of bop. In 1945 he played with Cat Anderson, and in '49 with Lester Young. He later gigged with Charlie Parker, Coleman Hawkins, and Stan Getz, and returned to Lester Young in '52.

In 1955, Kay replaced Kenny Clarke in the famous Modern Jazz Quartet. He recalled his introduction to their music: "I went to see the MJQ at Birdland," says Kay. "Kenny quit that night. They had a gig the next night, so they called me in the morning and asked me to work on upcoming gigs. I was just filling in until they got somebody steady. But I stayed. I could see the future in the MJQ. I *knew* they were going to happen."

One of the most popular groups in the history of jazz, the MJQ combined elements of jazz and classical, and remained together continuously until 1974. Throughout those years, Kay would rightfully gain a reputation as one of the most unobtrusive yet authoritative players on the scene. Noted for his delicate use of triangles, crotales, miniature timps, and other percussion instruments, Kay's performances were the epitome of clean, sensitive drumming.

"A lot of people think the MJQ's music is mechanical—that it's all written out," said Kay. "We do have a format, but after I get that together and stop looking at the chart, there's room for expression and ideas. When I first joined, John [Lewis] used to write a lot of notes in the drum part. But after I was there awhile, he hardly wrote anything for me unless it was something very specific. With this kind of music, you can get it technically right on paper, but it might not be exactly what you want. It's up to the *player* to bring it out."

Between the years of the MJQ's breakup and eventual reuniting in 1981, Kay spent four years with Benny Goodman, worked as house drummer at Condon's in New York, and performed on a wealth of recordings. Along with the dozens of Modern Jazz Quartet albums, Kay can be heard with Bobby Timmons, Randy Weston, John Coltrane, Cannonball Adderley, Herbie Hancock, Sonny Stitt, Gerry Mulligan, Sonny Rollins, Red Norvo, and Tommy Flanagan.

Connie Kay brought a sophistication to jazz drumming rarely heard before. His restraint and subtle use of varied tone colors were clear proof that jazz drumming could indeed be penetrating and driving, as well as lyrical and intelligent.

"Connie is like a security officer. He gives you a sense of balance and makes you feel secure." —Richard Davis

Ed Thigpen

A knowledgeable and well-schooled player, Ed Thigpen was a formidable spokesman for the early '60s breed of thinking man's drummer. Thigpen was born in Chicago in 1930, the son of drummer Ben Thigpen, who'd been with Andy Kirk's band from 1930 to '47. Starting out on piano, Thigpen switched to drums during the fourth grade, studied with Ralph Collier, and took his first professional job at the age of 18 with reed player Buddy Collette. During the '50s and '60s, Thigpen played with three of the jazz world's most revered pianists: Bud Powell, Billy Taylor, and Oscar Peterson, and clearly recalls each experience:

On Powell: "I worked at Birdland with Bud, with Charles Mingus on bass. Mingus started prodding me for more independence. Of course, I was trying to concentrate on Bud. I *knew* what Mingus wanted, but I couldn't do it because I had to do it the way *I* felt it was going to work. It never worked for me to try to sound like this guy or that guy."

On Taylor: "I can't say enough about the guy. Billy had a great deal to do with solidifying my ideas. I learned to appreciate the beauty of ballads and the harmonic aspects of music. I learned about all the subtle things you can do with the instrument, like how to use colors that blend harmonically, and how to pull it all together."

On Peterson: "That trio was a little orchestra. Every tune had to be an opener and a closer. We had a philosophy that we were going to play *so good* every night that even on a bad night, we'd be head and shoulders above everyone else. Ray [Brown] and I would wake up in the morning and practice time. We'd practice dynamics, tempos, and singing the tunes we played."

Thigpen stayed with Peterson until 1965, and next joined singer Ella Fitzgerald. After moving to Los Angeles in '67, he worked with Peggy Lee, Johnny Mathis, Oliver Nelson, and Gerald Wilson, and did free-lance studio work. In '68, Thigpen re-joined Fitzgerald, where he remained until moving to Europe, where he's worked steadily ever since with artists like Kenny Drew, Hank Jones, Ernie Wilkins, Dorothy Donegan, and Teddy Wilson, among others. Thigpen has also taught at The Music Conservatory in Denmark since 1974, performed with his own group, and appeared as a sideman with virtually every important American jazz figure at major European jazz festivals each year. Recognized for his superb taste, impeccable time, and outstanding facility with brushes, Ed Thigpen has maintained a reputation as one of the most articulate jazz drummers in the business.

> "Being the drummer in the Peterson trio was like being a jockey with a great race horse."
> —Ed Thigpen

Joe Morello

Internationally acclaimed author/teacher George Lawrence Stone once said about Joe Morello, "I consider him to be one of the most talented executants I have ever heard. In addition to speed and control, he has the most highly developed sense of rhythm and feeling for jazz, without which all other endowments fail."

Morello was born in Springfield, Massachusetts in 1928 and started out on the violin at age five. Switching to drums at 12, with aspirations of being a classical percussionist, Morello studied with Joe Sefcik, and later with George L. Stone and Billy Gladstone. Arriving in New York in 1952, he initially worked with guitarist Johnny Smith, and then briefly with the Stan Kenton band. In 1953 he joined the Marian McPartland trio at the Hickory House, where he remained for the next three years.

In 1956, Morello began his 12-year association with the popular Dave Brubeck Quartet. "When I first joined we didn't rehearse," said Morello. "He sent me a couple of records and said, 'Memorize a few of these tunes.' They had these tricky little polyrhythmic things where they'd go into three, then four, then two. But it was simple for me because I used to do that in Springfield. Now, when I listen to the things we used to do, they sound so simple. But not too many people were doing that kind of thing back then. It had some real good moments."

Throughout his career, Morello has revealed an exceptional sense of swing and finesse combined with astounding technical ability. Thousands of aspiring drummers were both awed and inspired by his technical facility. Along with witty and inventive solo work, Morello was extremely adept at negotiating odd time signatures, an ability that was finely honed during the Brubeck years.

Though long admired as a great all-around player and a skilled technician, Morello expressed his views on technique in an *MD* interview with Rick Mattingly: "Technique is only a means to an end. It opens your mind and you can play more intricate things. The more control you have the more confidence you get, and the more you're able to express your ideas. But technique alone—forget it! Just to see how *fast* you play doesn't make any sense. If you can't use it musically— if you're just going to machine gun everyone to death—that's not it."

Throughout his illustrious career, Morello has displayed a rare combination of drumming talents, all of which have made him one of the most revered players of all time. Since leaving Brubeck, Joe Morello has continued to perform with his own quintet, and has become one of the most in-demand teachers in the country.

"He moves gracefully, but with a sparkling, diamond-sharp attack reminiscent of Sid Catlett."
—Marian McPartland

Ed Blackwell

Influenced by New Orleans drummers Paul Barbarin, Zutty Singleton, and Baby Dodds, Ed Blackwell proved to be one of the most versatile and musical drummers to come out of the '60s. Blackwell's drumming career began in New Orleans during the late '40s. Blackwell is best-known for his landmark work with avant-garde saxophonist Ornette Coleman, whom he met in New Orleans in 1949. After the drummer moved to California in '51, the two renewed their association and began performing together in 1953.

Blackwell recalled his early encounter with the music of Ornette Coleman: "We started playing together because he couldn't find anybody else to play with," remarked Blackwell. "Nobody wanted to play with him. I thought that was amazing. Here was this cat playing all this music, and *nobody* wanted to play with him."

Following his stay in California, Blackwell returned to New Orleans for the remainder of the '50s, prior to moving to New York in 1960 to once again play in Coleman's quartet, replacing Billy Higgins. "A lot of people weren't aware that Ornette and I had played together before," said Blackwell. "Everybody was telling Ornette, 'Man, you ain't gonna get a drummer to play that shit.' He was telling them, 'I know somebody who can play it.'"

Reflecting on Coleman's music, Blackwell remembers, "Ornette would start off with 1 here, and the next time 1 would be somewhere else. So you had to listen to where he put that 1 to follow where it was. If you were going by where *your* 1 was, and you were playing that AABA form, it just wouldn't work!"

In his solo work, Blackwell was noted for setting up counter-rhythms between his hands and feet. However, his concepts were always deeply rooted in melodic drumming. "That started to develop when I began listening to Max," says Blackwell. "The way Max developed melodic lines along the structure of the tunes, I just enhanced it more by playing with Ornette. But I had a good concept of how to play a solo along a structured tune. I never had any preconceived ideas of the way I wanted to play any tune. I would just adapt to the way the tune was going, and adapt my playing to the way I heard the music."

A lifelong student of African rhythms, Ed Blackwell has remained among the most prolific players of the post-bop era. Along with Coleman, he's performed with Don Cherry, John Coltrane, Eric Dolphy, Booker Little, Randy Weston, Mose Allison, Albert Heath, and Archie Shepp, and has taught in the jazz department of Wesleyan University in Connecticut.

> "He really impressed me because I had never heard anyone play drums like that."
> —Billy Higgins

Billy Higgins

Billy Higgins was born and raised in Los Angeles, and began his career playing in R&B bands on the West Coast. He credits Max Roach, Kenny Clarke, Art Blakey, and Frank Butler as his primary sources of inspiration, though his musical influences ran well beyond drummers. "Most of my influences came from other instruments," Higgins has said. "I used to listen to Art Tatum, Bud Powell, Charlie Parker, and Milt Jackson for that kind of conception. You listen to people like that and figure you can also imply melody on *your* instrument. Drums are the hardest instrument to get music out of. You can play a lot of rhythms, but it's the hardest because you don't have that much to work with. So you've got to be thinking that way."

In 1959, Higgins went to New York as a charter member of the Ornette Coleman group, whose live performances and recordings had a profound effect on the jazz world: "Ornette was writing a lot of music, and we started playing together and learning. Ornette never said anything but, 'Play your heart out!' He left it up to you. When somebody has *that* much confidence in you, you have to come up with something. He was just so wide open. Whatever you wanted to do was okay. If you didn't feel like playing, you didn't have to play. We didn't have any music on the bandstand. Once you start playing together a lot you start breathing together, and then it becomes natural. It's something that becomes a part of you, and it becomes so natural that it's no mystery."

Later in his career Higgins played with Thelonious Monk, John Coltrane, Lee Morgan, Jackie McLean, and Hank Mobley, and he spent three years with Sonny Rollins. His work with Coleman continued on and off over the years, while he performed in trios and quartets with Cedar Walton and Clifford Jordan, touring Europe and Japan. Equally at home with traditional boppers or modernists, and possessing a highly individualistic style, Billy Higgins can be heard on hundreds of recordings with such artists as Dexter Gordon, Jimmy Heath, Barry Harris, Charles McPherson, Jimmy Raney, Pat Martino, Curtis Fuller, and Mal Waldron.

Commenting on his role in the evolution of jazz drumming, Higgins has said, "I'm glad I'm able to play music and be a link in the chain. Jazz is a family. It's a blessing just to be a *part* of it, because there are so many and it's a big family. I'm just trying to keep up the tradition."

"The music was always the challenge, regardless of who it was."
—Billy Higgins

Dannie Richmond

As the restraints of bar lines and tempos began to loosen, the jazz drummer's capacity to respond became extremely important, and drummer Dannie Richmond matured into one of the most responsive players of the '60s.

Richmond was born in New York in 1935, and as a teenager, he played tenor sax in rock 'n' roll bands. With the exception of several side ventures, and a host of free-lance work, Richmond was primarily known in jazz circles for his *important* contribution to the music of Charles Mingus, with whom he worked from 1956 to '70, and again from 1974 to '79. As an inspirational member of the Mingus Dynasty, Richmond adapted his style so that it perfectly complemented the abstract concepts of Mingus's music. His interpretation of the complexities of the music involved continual experimentation with flexible time and extended forms of improvisation, and his drumming was notable for stretching the boundaries of modern jazz through rhythmic and melodic interplay. Always willing to take great risks within the context of Mingus's approach to jazz, Richmond's provocative drumming abounded with fresh concepts and original thinking.

Dannie Richmond was also versatile enough to handle other types of music on an equally high level. Following his 14-year stint with Mingus, he spent three years performing and recording with the Mark-Almond band. Richmond also worked with Joe Cocker, toured with Elton John, and led his own quartet. In 1974, he returned to the Mingus drum chair, where he remained until the famed bassist's death in 1979.

Later, Richmond was part of a quartet that featured saxophonist George Adams, pianist Don Pullen, and bassist Cameron Brown. During the remaining years of his life he performed with Lew Tabackin and Benny Wallace, however, the Pullen/Adams quartet was regarded as his most *notable* post-Mingus venture. When not on the road, Richmond also gave drum clinics at colleges and high schools, and authored a method book published in Germany. Dannie Richmond passed away in 1988, but examples of his unique approach are preserved on numerous recordings with the Mingus Dynasty and with other influential jazz artists.

"Dannie was a very passionate person, and that was reflected in his playing."
—Cameron Brown

Ed Shaughnessy

Ed Shaughnessy was born in Jersey City, New Jersey, and began drumming at the age of 14. Ed was a frequent visitor to New York's 52nd Street music scene as a teenager, and it was there that he was befriended and influenced by Big Sid Catlett, which Ed fondly recalled in an *MD* interview with Robyn Flans. "Sid shaped my playing more than anybody," said Shaughnessy. "He could do it all. He had one of the most infectious pulses ever. Another reason he was so great was that he had a fantastic touch. A lot of people say I look graceful when I play. I think that has a lot to do with having seen Sidney. That was my first impression about how to play drums."

Shaughnessy's first professional job was with Jack Teagarden, which led to a two-year stay with tenor saxophonist Charlie Ventura. By the age of 21, Shaughnessy was performing with bandleader Tommy Dorsey as a replacement for Buddy Rich. Over the years he has also worked with George Shearing, Bobby Byrne, Benny Goodman, and Lucky Millinder, and has performed with The New York Philharmonic, the NBC and Pittsburgh symphonies, and bands led by Count Basie, Duke Ellington, and Oliver Nelson.

Shaughnessy was a popular figure in the New York recording studios for many years, and was one of the youngest musicians to be hired by CBS as a staff player, where he worked for five years. Building a solid reputation as a competent, versatile player, Shaughnessy then became a regular member of the NBC *Tonite Show* Orchestra, where he has spent the past 27 years.

"Contrary to what many people think, it wasn't the money that made me do studio work at a young age," said Shaughnessy. "It was the fact that I could still play *creative* music and be home. The jazz jobs then weren't always there, and when you worked at Birdland it was $90 a week. But it's actually been enjoyable the entire time. I consider myself a fortunate person. I'm playing with one of the really great big bands, and I haven't had to get on a *bus* to do it."

Shaughnessy has also fronted his own big band and small group, studied Indian drumming with Alla Rakha, and maintained an active schedule as a teacher and clinician. Among one of the most technically proficient drummers performing today, Ed Shaughnessy stands as a true champion of jazz and the education of young drummers.

"I always lived to play music; I didn't play music to live."
—Ed Shaughnessy

Billy Hart

"**I**n all the major innovative bands, the drummer has been totally free," said Billy Hart, one of the most dynamic of the new breed of players rising to prominence during the '60s. "Whether it was Baby Dodds with King Oliver, Jo Jones with Basie, Max with Bird, Philly Joe with Miles, or Elvin with Coltrane, the major innovators had the foresight to let the drummer be free."

Billy Hart was born in Washington, D.C. in 1940 and was attracted to jazz after hearing Charlie Parker on record. Basically self-taught, he credits Shadow Wilson, Sid Catlett, Max Roach, Art Blakey, and Philly Joe Jones as his primary influences.

Hart's professional career began with vocalist Shirley Horn, with whom he spent three and a half years. He later worked with Jimmy Smith and with famed guitarist Wes Montgomery, until Montgomery's death in 1968. Hart also performed on and off with Eddie Harris, Pharoah Sanders, and Marian McPartland, prior to joining Herbie Hancock's group for three years. He later worked with McCoy Tyner and Stan Getz, and in 1974 won *down beat* magazine's Talent Deserving Of Wider Recognition Award.

Billy Hart's drumming style was aptly described by Dave Liebman in the forward to Hart's book on jazz drumming. "Billy Hart represents something more than merely being one of the great drummers of jazz. He is a musician first and foremost who views the drums as part of the whole. His conception of time goes far beyond the pure function of timekeeping, and into the realm of musical color. That's one reason why he considers himself primarily a cymbal player, which translates into his ability to sustain sound longer than most drummers.

"Billy also reacts to harmony and melody throughout the drumset," continued Liebman. "He is keenly aware of the use of space, and often will only play part of a rhythmic figure instead of stating the entire configuration. When he fills the spaces between ideas offered by both the soloist and other rhythm section members, he is thinking in orchestral terms, coloring and shading the entire music. One of the obvious results of these concepts is the extended range of dynamics and constant variety of texture he uses when he plays. His major influences are the spiritual quality and conviction of John Coltrane's music, and the incredible pioneering and influential legacy of Max Roach."

Hart remains active on the jazz scene today and has released several albums as a leader.

"**I want the listener to feel the 'physicality' of nature surrounding us: the wind, the rain, and the sun.**"
—Billy Hart

William "Beaver" Harris

Beaver Harris was born in Pittsburgh in 1936, and studied with Pittsburgh Symphony percussionist Stanley Leonard, and with Kenny Clarke and Dante Augustini in Paris. Harris began his career with local bands around the Pittsburgh area following his Army discharge, and came to New York in 1962 to work with Sonny Rollins, Thelonious Monk, Joe Henderson, and Freddie Hubbard. In '67, Harris began his association with tenor saxophonist Archie Shepp, and soon established a reputation as one of the leading avant-garde drummers.

"My free playing had definite fundamental drum techniques in it," said Harris. "I wasn't just a free player who played without having full control over what I wanted to do. I developed my technique, and I'd always think very musically. What I'm really doing is taking the fundamental way of playing and expanding on that. I'm also continually singing melodies and counter-melodies, which is allowed in free playing. I had definite *foundations* for my free playing."

During his career Harris also worked with Albert Ayler, Gato Barbieri, Marion Brown, Roswell Rudd, and Steve Lacy, and for three years with pianist Cecil Taylor, replacing Andrew Cyrille. Towards the end of the '60s, Harris formed the 360 Degree Music Experience with Dave Burrell, Roland Alexander, Ron Carter, and Grachan Moncur III. Though the personnel has been altered over the years, Harris has continued to front the band off and on. "We wanted to get a band that could play any type of improvisational music," said Harris. "I decided to try different types of instrumentation. The purpose was to get as *much* out of the music as we could with the different combinations. We wanted to play everything from Scott Joplin to avant-garde."

Along with some of the jazz world's leading avant-garde players, Harris has also worked with Lee Konitz, Eddie Gomez, Jim Hall, Chet Baker, and Larry Coryell. A versatile drummer at ease in various genres, Harris elaborated on performing with musicians who represented different approaches to jazz: "I think of each player as a personal sound. I change up for each individual. If I'm playing with Archie Shepp, I think of a heavier sound. I almost lead him into things. If I play with Sonny Rollins, I try for a more musical sound. You've got to know how each person sounds and feels, and that's what you give to the music. You give it that feeling you receive."

> **"I've been able to play in all different forms of music because of the freedom I got from the avant-garde."**
> **—Beaver Harris**

Mel Lewis

A master of subtlety and understatement, Mel Lewis pioneered the small group approach to big band drumming with acute musical sensitivity. Taking a totally supportive position, Lewis acted as the cushion on which the band would rest. Never the technician, he made up for it with an instinct for blending with the band, coloring an arrangement, and maintaining dynamic control. "I learned that the power of drums was in this smooth glide of rhythm—not in volume," said Mel Lewis.

Lewis was born in Buffalo, New York in 1929, and was playing professionally by the age of 15. Over the years he worked with bands led by Lenny Lewis, Boyd Raeburn, Alvino Rey, Tex Beneke, and Ray Anthony, and in 1954 achieved National prominence with the Stan Kenton band. After moving to Los Angeles in '57, Lewis worked with Terry Gibbs and Gerald Wilson, among others, and co-led a band with arranger Bill Holman. In '62 he toured Russia with Benny Goodman, and returned the following year to work with Gerry Mulligan's band in New York. In 1965, Lewis teamed with trumpeter/arranger Thad Jones to form the Thad Jones/Mel Lewis big band. The band recorded, toured, and performed Monday nights at New York's Village Vanguard for years, and became one of the most popular big bands in the country.

A jazz purist, Lewis was known for using calfskin heads and old K Zildjian cymbals, both of which provided his trademark sound. "I always saved my Chinese cymbal for the hardest-blowing soloist," said Lewis. "I wanted to have a low cymbal behind a soloist with a harsh, high sound. With a subdued player with a softer edge, I didn't want something that strong, so I went to a lighter, higher sound to complement it."

In 1978, Thad Jones left the band, but Lewis kept it going, remaining at the helm up until his death in 1990. Regarded as one of the most musical big band drummers who ever lived, Lewis discussed in an *MD* interview the small group concept as it applied to big band playing.

"I actually started out as a small group drummer," said Lewis. "My favorite drummers had all come out of small groups. I loved big band drumming, but it seemed to me that it was awfully ponderous. I was so wrapped up in bop, that when I got with a big band, almost unknowingly I was throwing in a lot of offbeat stuff. I started using the ride cymbal when most big band drummers were still 'hi-hatting' away. I had my chance when I joined Kenton. I was kicking all over the place and playing exactly the same way I played with a small group. That was the first time I became aware myself that I had actually created a new thing."

"One of the really great big band players—Mel had the talent to make it all work."
—Stan Levey

"Mel didn't sound like anyone else."
—Buddy Rich

Mickey Roker

Mickey Roker was born in Miami in 1932 and raised in Philadelphia, where he started out playing R&B dates. In 1959 he worked with saxophonist Gigi Gryce in New York and quickly became a prominent figure on the jazz scene. Roker free-lanced with numerous artists through the '60s, and became one of the elite stable of players on the legendary Blue Note sessions.

"Each record date we did was fun, but it was also *serious* business," said Roker, recalling the golden age of Blue Note. "We'd rehearse for two days first. Engineer Rudy Van Gelder really knew how to get a good sound from people. He made it sound like you were listening to jazz live in the clubs. It was a beautiful experience for me, and I got to play with a lot of musicians."

Roker later spent two years with singer Nancy Wilson, and another two with Duke Pearson's big band prior to working with trumpeter Lee Morgan from 1969 to '71. Roker came to the attention of serious jazz listeners with Dizzy Gillespie's band, with whom he worked for nine years. Roker recalled the experience for *MD* interviewer Jeff Potter:

"Dizzy was always giving directions and whispering things in your ear. He likes you to try things. He'll give you a rhythm, but he wants you to take that rhythm and wring it out—put the accent here, the accent there—so that you exhaust the possibilities. And each time you'd play the rhythm, you'd find something new. This guy has played with the greatest drummers in the world, so it was like going to school."

Roker has also performed with Ella Fitzgerald, Oscar Peterson, Sam Jones, Wes Montgomery, and Milt Jackson. Among one of jazz drumming's more versatile players, he's recorded with Herbie Hancock, Horace Silver, Joe Williams, Zoot Sims, McCoy Tyner, Art Farmer, Nat Adderley, and Sonny Rollins. Commenting on the versatility that has kept him high on the list of the most in-demand drummers, Roker states, "You've got to listen to the players who do various styles authentically, and keep an open mind. You can't be a musical snob. I played Dixieland and blues, though I prefer playing bebop. But to make a living you have to be able to play *anything*. You never know when you're going to be called upon to play something other than what you like yourself."

"People can feel my playing, and they know it's me. That's what I want. That's what I try to do."
—Mickey Roker

Andrew Cyrille

"I'm there to make an event, a happening. If it's not an event, I feel as though I haven't arrived," said Andrew Cyrille, one of the most innovative of the avant-garde drummers of the '60s.

Cyrille was born in Brooklyn in 1939 and studied with Lennie McBrowne and Philly Joe Jones. "Joe took me under his wing and talked to me about drumming and music," recalled Cyrille. "He'd let me go to a lot of those record sessions he was on, and sometimes on jobs he'd let me sit in with the older musicians. That was an experience."

After attending the Juilliard School for a brief period, Cyrille gained his early playing experience with Duke Jordan, Cecil Payne, Nellie Lutcher, and Roland Hanna. By the early '60s he was performing with Walt Dickerson, Bill Barron, Roland Kirk, Jimmy Guiffre, and Cedar Walton. However, Cyrille's most important musical association came in 1964, when he joined pianist Cecil Taylor, with whom he remained until 1975. Taylor offered Cyrille an opportunity to fully express himself as a player, an experience he relayed in a 1981 *MD* interview:

"My role with Cecil was interpretive. Sometimes I'd be accompanying, but other times I'd be soloing simultaneously with the featured soloist, listening to what was happening around me. I'd think of forming contrasting shapes, sounds, and rhythms by employing various timbres from the set. I'd think of antiphonal phrasings. It was a push-pull concept that would suggest and absorb the ideas being presented. Sometimes I'd project certain feelings and pulses by using parts of the set in a particular way. For instance, I'd use the ride cymbal with alternate hand accents around the set to give a feeling of floating and levitation—or rapid, high-tension rhythms with incredible energy to generate force. Other times I'd suggest space, brevity, and peace, giving the feeling of being soothed. Whether the tempos were exceptionally fast or very slow, we struggled for sonic beauty with clarity of thought."

Along with his work with Taylor, Cyrille also played with Stanley Turrentine, Gary Bartz, Junior Mance, and Benny Powell. In the early '70s he led his own quartet, and later formed Dialogue of the Drums, a percussion trio with Milford Graves and Rashied Ali. Cyrille has also recorded with Coleman Hawkins, Marion Brown, Jimmy Lyons, and Grachan Moncur III. A complete musician, Andrew Cyrille has taught at Antioch College, has had his compositions performed at the Harlem Cultural Center, and continues to pass along his drumming expertise through an active private teaching schedule.

> "I think of sound, of colors, of rhythm. There are many different ways of approaching the drumset."
> —Andrew Cyrille

Elvin Jones

"I knew it sounded complicated, but it was only the appearance of complication," said Elvin Jones, the most influential jazz drummer of the '60s. "I wasn't status quo, but I didn't feel that it was all that different. It just didn't seem logical to me that the music we were playing could be approached any other way and still have logical conclusions. I grew up with the old methods and I learned them, and then I had to reject them. I chose to use the parts of them that suited me. I think it's an improvement. It adds more responsibility to the drummer, but it also offers greater opportunities."

Elvin Jones was born to a musical family in Pontiac, Michigan in 1927, then moved to New York in 1956 after spending several years with local Detroit bands. Shortly after his arrival in New York he began to work with Harry Edison, Donald Byrd, Bud Powell, Pepper Adams, and Sonny Rollins. In 1960 he joined the John Coltrane Quartet, a collaboration that would make musical history, while establishing Elvin Jones as one of the most creative voices in the history of jazz drumming.

"That Coltrane group gave me a whole new universe of possibilities to explore," recalled Jones. "It certainly was one of the most *significant* things that ever happened to me. It gave me such a clear insight into myself and my approach to music. It's a beautiful thing when you can use the knowledge you have and apply it in a context that works. It was the individuals that made it such a perfect situation for the drums—and for me as the controller of the instrument."

Elvin Jones' dynamic drumming encompassed many diverse elements that included complete four-limb independence, the variation of tone colors, and a unique sense of phrasing. His explorations of polyrhythmic devices, superimposition of meters—and the further subdivisions of those meters—had never been heard before. Jones' constantly altered ride cymbal patterns, unpredictable bass drum explosions, shifting accents, daring use of triplet figurations and open double-stroke rolls, and solos that incorporated ingenious use of tension and release, all became his personal trademarks. Though his time feel was basically relaxed, Jones was capable of producing a super-human rhythmic energy, and supplying an undercurrent that would drive Coltrane to amazing improvisational heights.

Since leaving Coltrane, Jones has led his own groups, which have included Joe Farrell, Wilbur Little, Jimmy Garrison, and Frank Foster, among others. With a unique, powerful approach that pointed jazz drummers in a totally new direction, Elvin Jones ranks high among the most important pivotal figures in the evolution of jazz drumming.

"People weren't aware of it until he got with 'Trane, but Elvin was always one of the masters."—Louis Hayes

"He breaks all the rules, but he has so much conviction and drive, that it all swings." —Jeff Watts

"Elvin's not just a drummer. He's a musical spirit." —McCoy Tyner

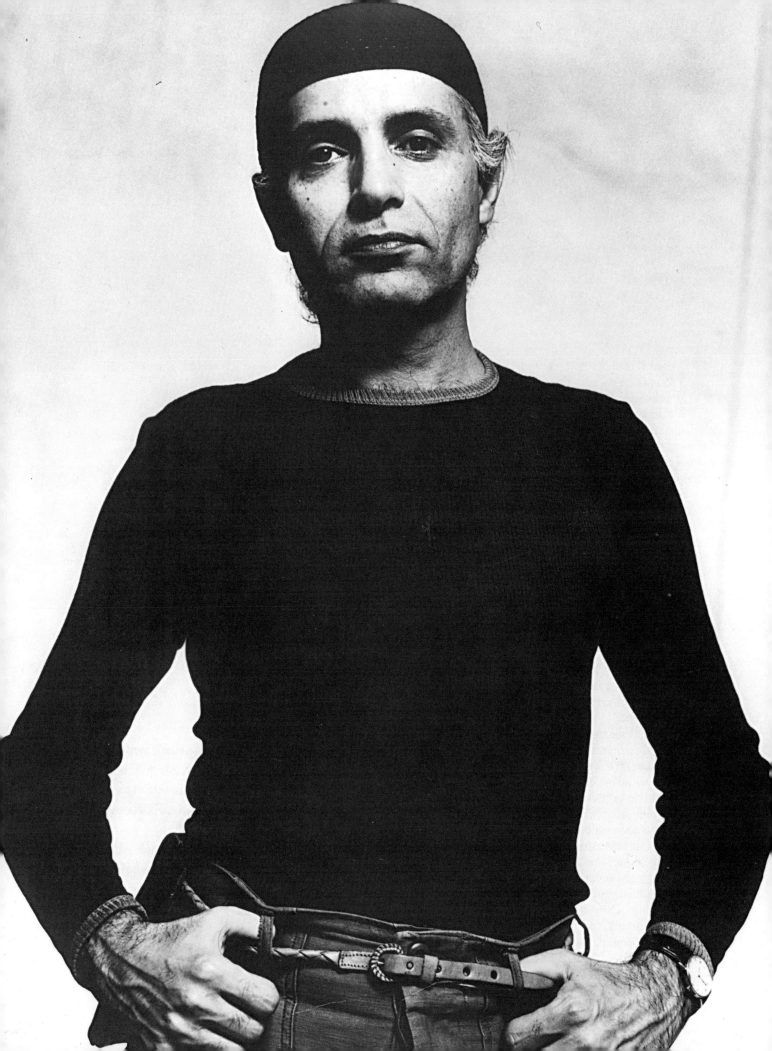

Paul Motian

Paul Motian was born in Philadelphia in 1931 and began playing drums at age 13. After studying with Billy Gladstone and at the Manhattan School of Music, where he studied timpani with Alfred Friese and Fred Albright, Motian began working around the New York area.

In 1959, he became affiliated with legendary pianist Bill Evans in the famed Bill Evans Trio featuring bassist Scott LaFaro, a group still considered to be among one of the finest of all time. "Bill and I used to play gigs together, and we lived in the same building," said Motian. "After Bill had been with Miles, he had his own trio and was playing at Basin Street. His drummer couldn't make it one night so he called me. Scott was playing around the corner and he came by and sat in. It seemed like that was it. Bill liked it a lot and we just kept it together. I played what I heard and tried to fit in with them. I never thought about playing that way. I've never pre-thought something. It seems like it's always been something that's happened through my involvement with the music and the musicians."

Though influenced during his formative years by Kenny Clarke and Max Roach, Motian's orchestral approach proved popular with many '60s modernists. In 1964 he worked with Paul and Carla Bley, and in 1966 he began his association with pianist Keith Jarrett. "I met Keith at a gig he was playing with Tony Scott, and he sounded great," said Motian. "Later on he called me and Charlie Haden, and we did Keith's first trio album. That was in '67. Later I played with Keith in Charles Lloyd's band."

Though recognized as one of the most contemporary players of the era with a free and aggressive drumming style, Motian still displayed an affinity for the tradition of drumming in an early *MD* interview: "I don't think a drummer or anyone else can just *start* playing 'free.' It comes from a tradition, and there's a lot involved. Musicians should check out the tradition of their instruments. There were so many really great drummers. People now don't know about Shadow Wilson, Kenny Clarke, Dave Tough, Chick Webb, Jimmy Crawford, and Baby Dodds. Their type of playing is connected with the way people are playing now. There's a certain art to playing the drums that's missing today."

A student of piano and composition, Paul Motian has also toured with Arlo Guthrie, led his own groups, recorded under his own name, and performed or recorded with Art Farmer, Thelonious Monk, Mose Allison, Tony Scott, Lee Konitz, Stan Getz, Don Cherry, and The Jazz Composers Orchestra.

"I learned a lot from Paul in terms of a freer, more open type of playing."
—Jack DeJohnette

Bob Moses

The free-spirited playing of drummer Bob Moses was once described by writer Charles Mitchell in this way: "Moses constantly searches for new colors, inflections, ways of dealing with tone and rhythm; free travel inside and out. Moses plays sonic alchemist, constantly keeping the cauldron at a low, intense boil."

Bob Moses was born in New York City in 1948 and began drumming at the age of 10. As a young drummer, his strongest influences were Max Roach and Dannie Richmond. By 1966 he was performing with guitarist Larry Coryell in a jazz/rock group called Free Spirits. In 1967, Moses played with Rahsaan Roland Kirk, and later spent two years with vibist Gary Burton. He has also worked with Steve Marcus, Dave Liebman, Randy Brecker, and drummer Jack DeJohnette in Compost. "We used to do double drum solos," recalls Moses on his association with DeJohnette. "Sometimes we'd play 40 minutes to an hour, just two drummers, and I wouldn't hold back anything. You can't peak or play your hardest before you finish because you won't be relaxed anymore."

A fluent performer with a highly original drumming style, Moses discussed his unique approach in an *MD* interview conducted in 1979. "It's not a technical thing as much as it is a conceptual thing. My playing gives the illusion of independence. But I don't use much independence. My playing is what I call the *dependent* style of drumming. I don't separate limbs by playing time with my right hand while my left does whatever it can against it. I'd never play a rhythm with just one hand or one foot. I use all four limbs constantly in a melodic fashion. I play the flow between my hands. If it's an 8th-note flow, I play 8th notes between two hands. I get the same effect because instead of putting both hands on the drum, I put the right hand on the ride cymbal so I get the feeling of a ride beat. And I put the right foot exactly with the right hand. It gives the cymbal sound a bottom. If I play at a really fast tempo, I don't catch every single beat. I pick the key ones I want to bring out. My right foot and left hand never stop. I'm not one of those drummers who can swing a band with just their right hand. I need *all* four limbs. That's why I call myself a dependent drummer."

An active teacher, composer, and author, Bob Moses is regarded as one of the most inventive players of the post-bop era.

"One of the most creative minds I've ever met among musicians."
—Gary Burton

Ben Riley

"The biggest impression came the night I heard Kenny Clarke," says Ben Riley. "I loved that he wasn't over the top of anyone, no matter who he played with. He uplifted the music without overpowering anyone."

Riley was born in Savannah, Georgia in 1933, and went on to play with most of the leading jazz artists from the mid-'50s through the mid-'60s, including Junior Mance, Ahmad Jamal, Sonny Rollins, Stan Getz, Roland Hanna, Eric Dolphy, John Lewis, Kenny Burrell, Sonny Stitt, Billy Taylor, Eddie "Lockjaw" Davis, and Johnny Griffin. However, Riley's place in jazz history was permanently secured during his three-year stay with jazz innovator Thelonious Monk. Riley offered an absorbing perspective on his relationship with Monk in a 1986 *MD* interview:

"Thelonious is one of the few composers whose music has to be played almost note for note to make it sound like it's supposed to sound. Most of his music plays itself. The beauty of it is the simplicity. Monk had a great sense of time and rhythmic construction. I played two or three different ways in that band until I felt comfortable. Certain tunes dictated that I find another way to interpret the beat. I got more into a Shadow Wilson style of playing later on, because it left a lot of space for the other musicians to do what they wanted. Monk's music also demanded that you become *involved*. Rather than just counting bars, you had to become melodically involved in it. Monk allowed me the freedom to enhance what was happening. He never played anything he didn't think a player could handle. He would play just enough music, and when he thought you were comfortable with that, he'd step up to other things that might be more intricate."

An extremely musical, melodic, and sensitive drummer, Riley went on to work with the New York Jazz Quartet in '71, and later with Alice Coltrane and Ron Carter's quartet. In 1984 he began his musical association with South African pianist/composer Abdullah Ibrahim. "Abdullah is from a different culture," states Riley. "There's an African drum influence, so you have to lay back and let that take precedence over what you do. I can't stay on top of the beat with him. The music demanded that I think and approach it in a different way."

Along with co-founding Sphere with Charlie Rouse, Kenny Barron, and Buster Williams, Riley has also performed over the years with Walter Bishop, Kai Winding, Woody Herman, Nina Simone, Milt Jackson, Toots Thielemans, and the Jim Hall Trio. Though somewhat lesser known than some of his contemporaries, Ben Riley remains among the most respected drummers in jazz.

"I try to keep aware of the aesthetic beauties around me. I guess that's why I play the way I do."
—Ben Riley

Al Foster

"The very first thing that really made me want to play drums was Max Roach's and Clifford Brown's 'Cherokee,'" recalls Al Foster. "After I heard Max, I really started checking out modern jazz. And Philly Joe—I know I got something from him. These are the guys I saw at a young age: Philly Joe, Art Blakey, Max."

Foster was born in Richmond, Virginia and moved to New York as a youngster. By the time he was a teenager, he was working in local clubs around New York. A versatile player, Foster soon came to the attention of major jazz artists, and gigs with Cannonball Adderley, Blue Mitchell, and Horace Silver followed. Finally, Miles Davis heard Foster in the early '70s at the Cellar Restaurant in New York, and asked him to join his jazz/rock group. It was the beginning of a musical relationship that would endure on and off for the next 13 years.

An inventive and original stylist, Foster was particularly noted for his outstanding hi-hat work with Davis. "Miles really loved the open hi-hat thing," recalls Foster. "He didn't like that tight, closed hi-hat groove. I suggested doing some of the tunes with a closed hi-hat many times, but he really didn't like it. Even if he would give me permission to try it, it wouldn't last a whole tune before he'd turn around and say something. He really fell in love with that open hi-hat. He said it sounded like a drone, a constant sound."

One of the most in-demand players of the post-bop era, Foster has also recorded or performed over the years with Sonny Rollins, Eddie Gomez, Michael and Randy Brecker, Joe Henderson, Bobby Hutcherson, John Scofield, McCoy Tyner, Freddie Hubbard, Carmen McRae, Kenny Barron, Branford Marsalis, Herbie Hancock, and Pat Metheny.

Perhaps the best description of Al Foster's playing was offered by writer Robin Tolleson in a rare *MD* interview: "Al doesn't play phrases you'd expect, or hit the instrument you'd expect him to hit at any given time. The things he plays aren't always expected, but they fit beautifully. Whether he introduces a persistent triplet figure on the cymbal while the rest of the band keeps right on the groove, or isolates the bass drum for some solo kicks while keeping the time going with his right hand, Foster forces his audience to sit up and *listen*. He doesn't merely lay it all right in their laps."

"You just try to contribute what you can. It's nice to know you've contributed something, small as it might be."
—Al Foster

Jack DeJohnette

"I took the preciseness of Tony and fused it with the looseness of Elvin and came up with Jack DeJohnette," said DeJohnette in an *MD* interview. Often described as a composer at the drumset, Jack DeJohnette's playing marked still another major move forward in the evolution of jazz drumming.

DeJohnette was born in Chicago in 1942, studied piano for 12 years, and took up drums at age 16. A graduate of the American Conservatory of Music, DeJohnette began his career in Chicago with blues bands, and with the free jazz of artists like Richard Abrams and Roscoe Mitchell. After arriving in New York in 1966, he worked with Jackie McLean, Betty Carter, and Abbey Lincoln, and for over two years in Charles Lloyd's quintet.

In 1970 DeJohnette joined Miles Davis, and for the next two years his powerful, intense drumming could be heard on some of Davis's most important recordings. "High intensity doesn't mean it's loud all the time," states DeJohnette. "No matter if it's a ballad or a fast tempo, it can have an intensity underlying the music that gives it a presence. You get energy and intensity from having an *intent* with your music. Intent, coupled with the concentration of focusing your energy."

An extremely musical player with an approach evolving from a strong mixture of bop and rock, DeJohnette's style oftentimes utilized all the components of the drumset to create a wash of rhythm that inspired soloists to incredible heights. "You don't have to keep the swing strictly on the cymbal," explained DeJohnette. "You can shift from the cymbal to the bass drum, or you can play something between the snare and tom. I always try to think of the drumset like a piano, with the cymbals being the sustain pedal. When you break up all these patterns around the set, you're just shifting the emphasis and tonal color, but there's always a connection. There's a rhythm going on *somewhere* in the complexity.

"I think of each hand and foot as a separate personality," continues DeJohnette. "I'll get dialogs going between the snare and bass drum, or with the cymbal. I'll bounce phrases around the different components of the set. Another way I look at it is thinking of the feet as two more hands, and using them for independent phrases, not just accents. I play whole phrases, which makes the drums sound fuller. I kind of give each component of the set equal time."

Over the years DeJohnette has also performed with John Coltrane, Thelonious Monk, Freddie Hubbard, Bill Evans, Keith Jarrett, Chick Corea, McCoy Tyner, Pat Metheny, Herbie Hancock, Sonny Rollins, and Stan Getz. An accomplished composer and pianist as well as a true drummer's drummer, Jack DeJohnette continues to be one of the most influential figures on the jazz scene.

"Jack sounds good in any situation—whether it's hard bop or anything else."
—Al Foster

"I love his looseness, his fluidity, and his very musical approach to playing drums."
—Dave Weckl

Rashied Ali

Known for his ability to devise complex, multi-directional rhythms—while allowing the soloist maximum freedom—Rashied Ali was among the more popular players in the '60s avant-garde circles.

Ali was born in Philadelphia in 1935, and worked locally with numerous bands throughout the '50s. His jazz career began in Philadelphia with McCoy Tyner, Lee Morgan, and the Heath Brothers. Ali was a student of Philly Joe Jones, and came to New York in the early '60s, where he was soon performing with avant-gardists Don Cherry and Pharoah Sanders. Jobs with other modernists like Paul Bley, Bill Dixon, and saxophonist Archie Shepp soon followed.

In 1965 Ali began performing with John Coltrane, playing alongside of Elvin Jones at the onset. "For the first six months or so we played together," recalled Ali. "Elvin left the band in California. Later we went to Chicago and picked up Jack DeJohnette. Then John started cutting down on the band, and finally it got down to just Alice [Coltrane], John, Jimmy Garrison, and me. We did a lot of recording like that. Musically, John found what he wanted to do, and he had broken it down to the kind of band he wanted."

Ali was Coltrane's last full-time drummer, moving on to play in Europe after Coltrane's death in '67. Since then he has led his own quartet, performed with the Afro Algonguin Trio, the Funkyfreeboppers, the Saheb Sarbib quintet, and Sonny Rollins. He has also recorded and performed with Jackie McClean, Bud Powell, and groups that have included modernists like Sonny Fortune, Odean Pope, and Calvin Hill.

One of the strongest of the free players, with a highly personal approach to the instrument, Ali's drumming was described by Harold Howland for *MD*: "He seems to rely little on the natural rebound of the surfaces, and jabs at his cymbals with quick, delicate strokes, usually clutching the stick intently with all his fingers. His drums are muffled well beyond accepted jazz standards, and his cymbals are tightened to the stands at a deep slant so they do not swing freely. He seeks a dark, understated tone quality in his cymbals and strikes them carefully. The feel of Ali's pulse is very much on top of the beat and highly intuitive. He will contrast turbulent bass drum figures and uproarious multi-cymbal washes with fills that consist of casual, sometimes barely audible roll patterns, in a way that suggests the natural, rather than the regulated passage of time."

"He could really propel Coltrane to some other heights."
—Jack DeJohnette

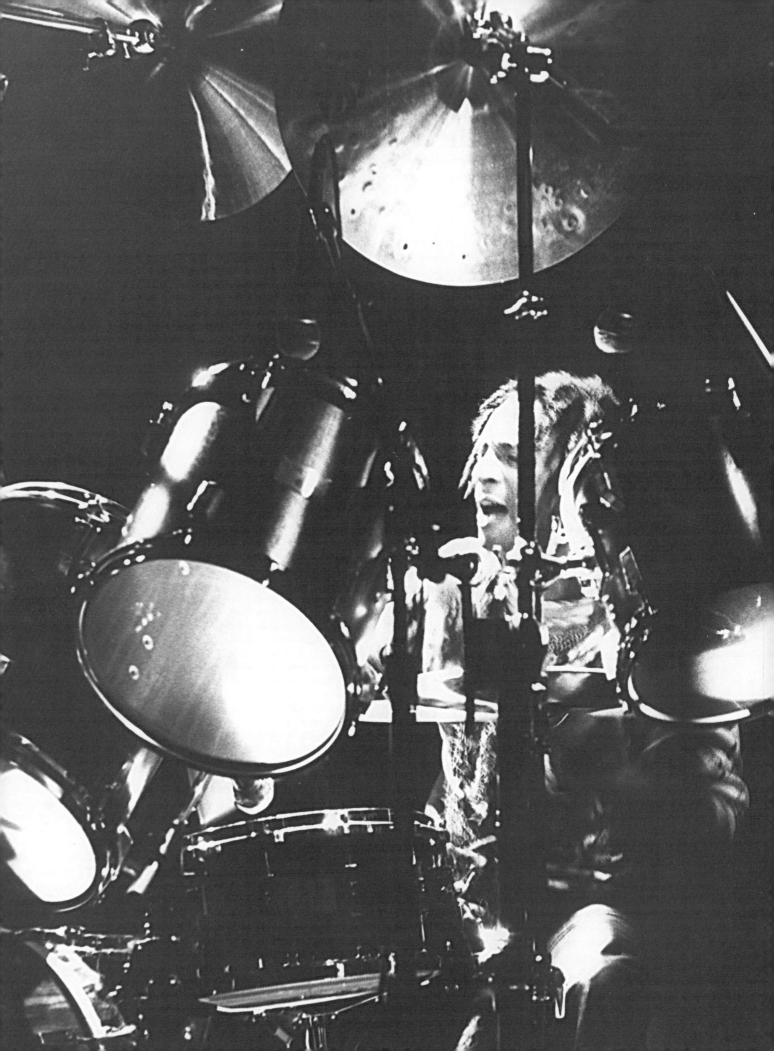

Ronald Shannon Jackson

Ronald Shannon Jackson is among the most distinctive of the avant-garde stylists. Writer Chip Stern's succinct description of Jackson's approach was offered in a 1984 *MD* interview:

"Jackson's drums are not simply the hip timekeeper, but the central core of the band's melody. They key the matrix of polytonalities he orchestrates as tonal extensions of his four limbs. Where McLaughlin (with Cobham) and Corea (with White) would deal in polymetric extensions of the melody, Shannon attempts a synthesis of elements more akin to the polyrhythmic modulations of African tribal drummers—a layering of different tempos, key centers, and cross-rhythms."

Jackson was born in 1940 in Texas and played in blues and dance bands before coming to New York to work with Junior Cook, Bill Hardman, Betty Carter, and Charles Mingus. Over the years Jackson was acclaimed for his work with Albert Ayler, Ornette Coleman, Cecil Taylor, and James Blood Ulmer, and presented insight on each experience:

On Ayler: "No one played with more power than Albert. Playing with him made me aware of where my rhythmic center was coming from—down in my gut. Once you're past the conscious level, everything is open and you can get to the music, not just your instrument. I began to get a sense that *real* drumming is about transcending, about making the music jell so the band functions as a unit."

On Coleman: "He'd never tell me what to play, and his music afforded me total freedom to play what I wanted. He'd just play the 'cool observer game' and see what you'd come up with. He expected you to come up with an appropriate part. Playing with Ornette taught me how to anticipate quickly."

On Taylor: "Working with Cecil gave me a lot in terms of structuring my ideas. Cecil's music has such a highly developed rhythmic structure. He would play things in 5, 7, 9, and 11, and all these other complex rhythms. I was able to incorporate my own rhythms into his thing and enhance what he was doing."

On Ulmer: "Playing with Blood was easy, because we both instinctively understood what the rhythmic concept was. While I was with him I began getting concepts for my ideal drumkit, and I started to come down off the cymbals onto the drums—which is something really hard for drummers to do."

Shannon later formed his own electric ensemble called the Decoding Society, and explained the purpose of the band's music: "I'm trying to unite people with the knowledge that music is a force, and to portray that element of swing in our era. Living in the present, and knowing about the past so we can anticipate tomorrow, is what I'm trying to do with the Decoding Society."

> "I'm making a statement that jazz is not dying, and is never going to die."
> —Ronald Shannon Jackson

Tony Williams

The art of modern jazz drumming made still another giant leap forward in the '60s with the arrival of Tony Williams, a young innovator who would ultimately change the face of jazz.

Williams was born in Chicago in 1945 and raised in Boston. He was a student of Alan Dawson at age 10, and by 15 was playing professionally with saxophonist Sam Rivers. Recognized as a true drumming prodigy, Williams' talent was promptly acknowledged among the elite of jazz drumming. "Max, Art, and Philly Joe were my first idols," recalled Williams. "I got to meet them when I was very young. They were like my big brothers. They were always very kind to me. It was a big help."

In 1962 Williams moved to New York to work with Jackie McLean, but was soon heard by Miles Davis, who quickly made him part of his quintet, which included Herbie Hancock, Ron Carter, and Wayne Shorter. As a member of one of the most innovative groups of the '60s (at age 17), Williams displayed an *astute* sensitivity for the musical concepts of Miles Davis.

Williams remained with Davis until 1969, and then formed the Tony Williams Lifetime featuring John McLaughlin and Larry Young. The band proved to be a unique blending of free jazz and high-energy rock, and paved the way for a whole generation of fusion bands. "On those first records with Lifetime, I was just trying to do something that no one else had done," said Williams. "I had been hearing things that other people had done and I thought, 'Wow, if they can do that, then I can do this.' That's how it came about."

In 1975, Lifetime was re-formed with guitarist Allan Holdsworth and keyboardist Alan Pasqua. Two of the band's recordings—*Believe It* and *Million Dollar Legs*—once again demonstrated the energy, technique, and taste of Tony Williams. Later Williams toured and recorded with V.S.O.P., with the Great Jazz Trio featuring Hank Jones and Ron Carter, and with Sonny Rollins and Weather Report.

Clearly the most influential jazz drummer of his time, Tony Williams' style was briefly described by *down beat* editor Don DeMichael: "He creates a screen of sounds—tinkled cymbals, crashes, ticks of sticks on wood, sudden splashes as he flicks off his hi-hat, blurred open rolls, and a series of off-beat accents that create the illusion of a different tempo, so intense that the tension from the building sound feels as if it will break your head before he lets the stretched time snap back into position."

Tony Williams brought to jazz a wealth of drumming innovations, and a dynamic solo style that was clean and precise, warm and sensitive, and overflowing with emotion. His status as a living legend is readily acknowledged by every serious student of jazz drumming.

"Tony doesn't play time—he plays pulse."
—Eric Dolphy

"He was always such a creative genius to me."
—Vinnie Colaiuta

"You can't help being influenced by people like Tony."
—Steve Gadd

Steve Gadd

The appearance of Steve Gadd in the early '70s represented state-of-the-art drumming that embodied a rare combination of creativity, energy, and exceptional musical sensitivity.

One of the most in-demand and admired players in contemporary music, Gadd was born and raised in Rochester, New York, where he studied drumming with Bill and Stanley Street. After attending the Manhattan School Of Music and the Eastman School in Rochester, Gadd soon became active in the recording studios of New York. "It's more than just the *playing*," said Gadd, reflecting on his studio drumming success. "It's understanding what the whole job is and wanting to do it. They hire you because they know you can play, and they know you can apply your ability to any situation without getting an attitude. It's your *attitude*, and your willingness to try and understand what it is they're really going for."

One of the most technically proficient players of the era, Gadd's highly original approach was soon emulated by scores of drummers, and placed him in great demand among artists like Carly Simon, Phoebe Snow, Carol King, Paul Simon, Patti Austin, Chuck Mangione, Nancy Wilson, George Benson, Joe Farrell, Steve Kahn, and David Spinozza, and groups like Steely Dan, Stuff, and Steps. "My idea is never to have any preconceptions," said Gadd. "I just try to be in the situation for the moment. I try to play the music without putting my initials on it. I approach everything by listening first and finding something to play without going in thinking I'm going to play something *before* I get there. The music guides you. You can't put your eyes before your ears. The key thing is listening."

During the '70s Gadd proved his ability as a fluent jazz player in exciting performances with keyboardist Chick Corea. "Chick's compositions are all written out," states Gadd. "He knows what he wants to a point where he can really explain it and get the most out of you. And he writes the music very clearly. He can write a good drum part. Most of the albums I did with Chick, like *Leprechaun* and *Spanish Heart*, were all live, with strings and horns."

An extremely versatile player who grew up playing bop, Steve Gadd's overwhelming influence significantly altered the direction of modern drumming. "If I am an influence, I hope I'm a good one," said Gadd. "I don't play to be an influence. I feel a responsibility to the music I play. Let's say, being responsible to the *music* is the first step in accepting responsibility for people coming up."

"Steve always means every note he plays."
—Will Lee

"He created such great drum parts to the pieces I wrote."
—Chick Corea

"The guy's a genius. One of the baddest drummers in the world."
—Al Foster

Peter Erskine

"Basically I play the music I play because it's the music I enjoy," said Peter Erskine. "I recognize certain obligations to tradition and taste, but the primary motivating factor for most artists, I think, is to satisfy themselves. The drumset is my craft—my life's work. Maybe deep down, I'm just a bebopper at heart."

Peter Erskine was born in 1954, studied with Alan Dawson as a youngster, attended the Stan Kenton Stage Band Camps, and at the age of 18 joined the Stan Kenton band. After three years with Kenton, Erskine attended Indiana University, where he studied with percussionist George Gaber. But after a year, he was back out on the road, this time with the Maynard Ferguson band. "I grew up listening to big band music, and it excited this thing inside me," recalled Erskine. "I think any kind of gig a drummer can take that has strong traditions built in is an invaluable learning experience. But I would always find myself feeling a little envious when I'd hear small-group drummers—guys who *really* played the stuff. I would think, 'That's the kind of drumming I *really* want to play.'"

Erskine later moved on to play with Weather Report, a jazz fusion band featuring Joe Zawinul, Wayne Shorter, Jaco Pastorius, and later percussionist Robert Thomas, Jr. "Rhythmically, the key to Weather Report was that there were two different time things going on," said Erskine. "There was this one beat that was really propulsive and chugging ahead, and then the backbeat, which was in half time. We'd have this jazz thing with the cymbal moving ahead, while the snare and bass drum were playing a half-time rock thing. It was a nice blend of contrasting rhythms. It moved a certain way. Weather Report was my *favorite* band. It always has been and always will be. I was very fortunate. It opened an incredible number of doors for me."

A precise, articulate player, Erskine is equally at home in fusion or straight-ahead bop, and has performed or recorded with Joni Mitchell, Joe Farrell, Joe Henderson, George Cables, Gary Peacock, Eliane Elias, Bob Berg, Don Grolnick, and Jan Garbarek, among many others. In 1986 he performed and recorded with John Abercrombie and with Bass Desires, and later re-joined Weather Report, re-formed as Weather Update. An in-demand clinician, recognized author, and well respected musician, Peter Erskine is a leader among the current generation of great jazz drummers.

"Guys like Peter are going to last a long time because what they're doing is pure and it's right."
—Louie Bellson

Marvin "Smitty" Smith

Marvin Smith was born in 1961 in Waukegan, Illinois, began playing drums at age 3, and later studied with Charlie Williams and Donald Taylor. He attended the Berklee College Of Music for two years, gigged around the Boston area, and then worked with singer Jon Hendricks. Devoted to the rich history of jazz drumming, Smith relayed his views in an MD interview:

"I relate what I would like to do with percussion back to drummers of the '20s and '30s, and the bands of Fletcher Henderson and Duke Ellington. Take a cat like Sonny Greer: He wasn't just playing drums, he was playing percussion. He had all sorts of wood blocks, temple blocks, chimes, bells, triangles, timpani—you name it. And he was *using* them. It wasn't just for show."

Recognized as one of the most impressive young drummers on the jazz scene, Smith has played with John Hicks, Bobby Watson, Slide Hampton, Benny Golson, Art Farmer, and Frank Foster. He has also performed with Dave Holland, Ron Carter, Henry Mitchell, Tom Pierson, Sonny Rollins, Branford Marsalis, and Terrance Blanchard.

Smith is noted for his unique sound, and he elaborated on the subject. "I always loved that deep sound—that jungle drum sound," said Smith. "With all due respect to Max and all those great drummers who tune real high and get a beautiful sound, I was just hearing a much deeper 'gutbucket' sound—that raw Art Blakey sound that just reached out and grabbed you. I just love that depth of tone. That's the sound I'm hearing for now, and I'm trying to capture that sound. I tune my toms lower than most drummers. There's just something about four tom-toms that I love. It gives me more of a tonal range. It helps me achieve a more realistic melodic sound, and gives me more of a sense of pitch."

Well aware of his responsibility to carry forward the tradition of the great masters to the new generation of players, Smith summed it up simply: "I just want to apply all the experiences I've had and all the things I've learned, and reflect them in my music. I would just like to communicate with other musicians and the general public, as well as make a contribution on my instrument—a contribution to music for people."

**"Smitty can go in any direction he wants. That cat can play."
—Kenny Washington**

Carl Allen

Another player to aggressively lead the way into the '90s with a swinging, interactive style was Carl Allen. Allen was born in 1962, left Wisconsin for New York in the early '80s, and within a short while was working with Freddie Hubbard. That experience later led to gigs with Jackie McLean, George Coleman, and Randy Weston.

Allen discussed the two distinctive approaches needed to work with artists like Freddie Hubbard and Randy Weston. "Freddie's the kind of player who wants you to be battling with him," said Allen. "You just have to be out there all the time. With Randy it's a little different. He kind of sets the mood for what's happening, and you just kind of deal with that mood. You help put some colors in there and try to shape what's going on, but it's more of a cooperative thing."

Since making his appearance on the New York jazz scene, Allen has recorded as a sideman with Donald Harrison and Terrance Blanchard, and as a leader with groups including Roy Hargrove, Kenny Garrett, Ira Coleman, Donald Brown, Vincent Herring, and Freddie Hubbard.

A skilled composer, as well as an active teacher and clinician, Carl Allen openly expressed his views on the art of jazz drumming in a recent *MD* interview. "When I play, I try to get things from other instruments," said Allen. "Monk had a certain way of playing that I really liked. Monk played piano like drums in a way. Dexter Gordon had a certain way of playing that I hear being applied to drums—same with Miles. I'm picking up on that. I try to hear *melody* and *movement* so that I can help shape tunes. For me it's about trying to get that forward motion happening. It's about what you play internally, not just externally. I'm always playing against something in my mind—whether it's a bass line or a piano player comping. I try to create this ongoing surface, this form of communication.

"I also don't like to be predictable. I don't want cats to say, 'Yeah, well here's beat 1, so I know you're gonna hit a crash cymbal there.' I get a kick out of being unpredictable, particularly when cats play like they're dependent on the drummer all the time. I think everybody should be mature enough to know where 1 is on their own. My job isn't to baby-sit you. It takes a certain amount of maturity to deal with this music."

"When you mature, you come to realize that there's a higher calling for this music."
—Carl Allen

Kenny Washington

"**S**winging in the illustrious, immaculate style of a Philly Joe Jones or Mel Lewis, Kenny brings his exacting standards to bear on every gig he plays," said Ken Micallef in an *MD* interview with Kenny Washington. "A true ensemble player, he is also an inspired soloist and a master of the lost art of brush playing. One is immediately struck by his ability to swing hard at any tempo or volume, and by his constant use of dynamics—a truly musical drummer."

Kenny Washington was born in Brooklyn, New York and studied with Rudy Collins and Dennis Kinney. Washington was influenced by the drumming of Vernell Fournier, and has worked with Benny Carter, Walter Davis, Bill Hardman, Lou Donaldson, Walter Bishop, Milt Jackson, Clark Terry, Betty Carter, Dizzy Gillespie, and Johnny Griffin.

A true brush stylist in the tradition of Papa Jo Jones, Washington offered some thoughts on the subject. "Learn to play brushes with the snares *off*," recommended Washington. "That's the prettiest sound you'd want to hear. Jo Jones always played with the snares off. That sound projects. I just go for what I've heard on those Ahmad Jamal records with Vernell Fournier. I learned from Mel Lewis that the old players were using calfskin heads, which gave a much warmer sound than plastic. People have told me my brush sound projects, but it's mainly because I grew up trying to get a calfskin sound on a *plastic* head."

Also known for his sensitive use of dynamics to shape the music, Washington reflected on backing vocalists, particularly his playing with singer Betty Carter. "With Betty I learned a lot about playing colors, about different shadings, and about control. Betty would play something like 'My Favorite Things' at a breakneck tempo. The tune would go on for about five minutes and then she'd call a ballad. I'd put the sticks down and my hands would still be shaking. The ballad would be so slow you could go to the bathroom between beats. Another thing that makes her gig hard is that she doesn't like drummers to play brushes on the snare drum—no *sweeps*. She wants to hear that cymbal with the hi-hat on 2 and 4. She wants that wide open space. It's hard to do that and make it really groove."

Very much in demand on the current jazz scene, Washington can be heard on over 80 albums with a host of artists, including Lee Konitz, Ralph Moore, Mike LeDonne, Joshua Breakstone, and Tommy Flanagan, to name a few. Committed to the rich heritage of jazz drumming, Kenny Washington has maintained the standards set by Max Roach, Art Blakey, and Philly Joe Jones.

> "Kenny's serious and he can play. He's a very advanced little cat."
> —Billy Higgins

Dave Weckl

"I may not play bop or straight-ahead like the traditionalists might think is authentic," says Dave Weckl, "but playing straight-ahead jazz was a big part of my youth."

Dave Weckl is an outstanding young player who has moved jazz drumming into the '90s. Weckl was born in 1960 in St. Louis, and began playing drums at the age of 8. Following high school, Weckl enrolled in the jazz studies program at the University of Bridgeport, where he studied with Randy Jones and Ed Soph, and later privately with Gary Chester. Influenced primarily by Rich, Cobham, Erskine, and Gadd, Weckl attained local recognition with New York bands like Nite Sprite and French Toast.

In 1983 Weckl performed on the Simon & Garfunkel reunion tour, where his crisp attack, finesse, and firm command of dynamics brought him to the attention of scores of admiring musicians. "I'm very involved in the whole dynamic concept," said Weckl. "A lot of people tend to sound monotonal—not enough dynamic contrast. There's a certain degree of dynamics you have to find that will make the motion happen—whether one accent on the bass drum should be a little softer, or perhaps certain notes should be outlined in a hi-hat 8th-note pattern. You have to find out what will make the pulse. Dynamics, to me, make music *happen*."

In 1985, after proving his ability as a powerful, sensitive player with superb musical instincts and flawless execution, Weckl joined Chick Corea's Elektric Band, where his live and recorded performances won him national recognition. "I grew up listening to Chick," said Weckl. "I got a feel for his phrasing when I was young. From the first rehearsal, it just hit—it popped immediately. As a drummer, it's one of the greatest gigs to have. To have no barriers and be as creative as you want. Actually, you can't do anything *but* that. The minute you take it easy and just play the notes, it's definitely known. You have to be going for it all the time."

Along with Chick Corea's Elektric and Akoustic bands, Weckl has also recorded with Peabo Bryson, Robert Plant, Michel Camilo, Tania Maria, Paquito D'Rivera, Richard Tee, Ronnie Cuber, Dave Matthews, Steve Kahn & Eyewitness, and the S.O.S. Allstars. "I spent a lot of time trying to grasp the bebop concept," said Weckl. "It's almost like Latin music in a way. There's this feel to it, the way it flows. It's something I admire and I like to do. I feel I've gotten better at it primarily from listening and playing with Chick. It's hard *not* to progress in that situation."

"Dave's a consummate musician who makes a meal out of perfection."
—Chick Corea

"What impresses me about Weckl is that he's got identification. You know it's him."
—Louie Bellson

Jeff Watts

With a style strongly rooted in bop, Jeff Watts fashioned his own dynamic, tasteful approach to jazz drumming. Watts was raised in the Pittsburgh area, began playing in elementary school, and later attended Duquesne University, where he became a skilled percussionist. Watts was introduced to jazz at the age of 18, and recently recalled the experience: "My first real introduction to jazz was a pair of records," said Watts, "*Where Have I Known You Before* by Chick Corea & Return To Forever, and *Thrust* by Herbie Hancock & the Headhunters. I had all the Billy Cobham albums, I was a Chick Corea freak, and I dug Lenny White. I liked Michael Walden, and I had all those Larry Coryell records."

Moving to Boston after two years at Duquesne, Watts enrolled in the Berklee School Of Music. "Once I got to Berklee, there were some players who could swing and a lot of people to play with," recalled Watts. "It was interesting. I also got to see Elvin, Roy, Max, Art, and Philly—all the foundation cats—and I loved it. I fell in love with the music and I began to develop a jazz mentality."

In 1982 Watts' career was firmly launched when he joined with Wynton and Branford Marsalis in the Wynton Marsalis Quintet, featuring pianist Kenny Kirkland and bassist Charnett Moffett. Watts recalled his initial contact with the music of the Marsalis quintet. "When they called me to do *We Three Kings*, I knew it was for real, and I began to think about how I should approach the music. They were starting to listen to some music I'd only touched on—the music of Miles Davis. I approached it the way Tony Williams plays, from a conceptual point of view. What I got from Tony was the way he phrases. He turns the phrase like a beat ahead of where a bebop drummer would hear it."

Interestingly, Jeff Watts puts an appropriate closing touch on this volume with his own perspective on all that's preceded him. "When I was at Berklee, I made tapes of Sid Catlett, Baby Dodds, Chick Webb, and Jo Jones. I checked out where they were coming from. And Kenny Clarke—he was ahead of his time. Another drummer who moved me was Art Blakey. He always was loving and supporting. Philly Joe, man, he was like *it* for me for a long time—still is. Roy Haynes is just great because he reacts to what's happening around him. And Max—I can't even express how much he means to me. He plays drums on such a high level. Billy Higgins is a cat who epitomizes the sheer joy of swing every time he plays. And I always dug Dannie Richmond. I try to play like him sometimes. Ed Blackwell plays some of the most musical solos I've ever heard. And Elvin—he transcends the instrument on every level. The mere fact that he can play something so complex and make it sound so hip and swinging is amazing to me.

"I think everyone should do as much study and research into this tradition as possible, so they can contribute to its *survival*."

"It's one thing to listen to a record, but it's another to see these men, and to see where the inspiration comes from."
—Jeff Watts

Photo Credits

Tony Williams, Max Roach, Ben Riley, Al Foster, Ed Blackwell, Elvin Jones, Philly Joe Jones, Shelly Manne: **By Tom Copi.**
Jeff Watts, Mickey Roker, Buddy Rich, Billy Higgins, Andrew Cyrille, Jack DeJohnette, Mel Lewis: **By Veryl Oakland.**
Ed Thigpen, Rashied Ali, Steve Gadd: **By Charles Stewart.**
Baby Dodds, Zutty Singleton, Sonny Greer, J.C. Heard, Ray Bauduc, Ray McKinley, Gene Krupa, Dave Tough, Tiny Kahn, O'Neil Spencer: **Courtesy Rutgers Institute Of Jazz Studies.**
Cliff Leeman, Dave Weckl: **Courtesy Avedis Zildjian Company.**
Art Blakey: **By Joost Leijen.**
Bob Moses: **By Howie Greenberg.**

Kenny Clarke: **By Ray Ross.**
Marvin Smith: **By Laura Friedman.**
Carl Allen: **By Joanne Johnson.**
Ronald Shannon Jackson: **By Chase Roe.**
Roy Haynes: **By Allison Perry.**
Billy Hart: **By Collin Davis/Shaida.**
Peter Erskine: **By Paul Natkin/Photo Reserve.**
Dannie Richmond: **By Kathy Sloane.**
Beaver Harris: **By Lona Foote.**
Kenny Washington: **By Ebet Roberts.**
Alan Dawson: **By Lissa Wales.**
Jimmy Cobb: **By Rick Mattingly.**
Shadow Wilson: **By Frank Driggs.**
Louie Bellson: **Courtesy Pearl Corporation.**

Sound Supplement Reference

Track 1
Baby Dodds: "Spooky Drums," *The Drums*: ABC/Impulse ASH-9272E

Track 2
Papa Jo Jones: "Doggin' Around" (Count Basie) *Smithsonian Collection of Classic Jazz:* Smithsonian Institution/Columbia PG-11891

Track 3
Sid Catlett: "Afternoon Of A Basieite" (L. Young) *The Drums:* ABC/Impulse ASH-9272B

Track 4
Gene Krupa: "Gene's Blues," *Krupa And Rich:* Clef Records MGC-684

Track 5
Buddy Rich: "Bugle Call Rag," *The Buddy Rich Big Band: Big Swing Face:* Pacific Jazz/Liberty ST-20117

Track 6
Kenny Clarke: "No Smokin'" (H. Silver) *The Drums:* ABC/Impulse ASH-9272A

Track 7
Max Roach: "Woodyn' You" (D. Gillespie) *Max Roach + 4:* Emarcy/Mercury MG-36098

Track 8
Shelly Manne: "If I Were A Bell" (F. Loesser) *Shelly Manne And His Men At The Manne-Hole:* Contemporary M3593/4

Track 9
Art Blakey: "Thermo" *Caravan: Art Blakey Jazz Messengers:* Riverside RM-438

Track 10
Philly Joe Jones: "Strut Time" (B. Golson) *Benny Golson Blues On Down:* Milestone M-47048

Track 11
Joe Morello: "Shortin' Bread" *Gone With The Wind, The Dave Brubeck Quartet:* Columbia CL 1347

Track 12
Mel Lewis: "Cherry Juice" (T. Jones) *Naturally, Mel Lewis And The Jazz Orchestra:* Telarc Digital DG-10044

Track 13
Elvin Jones: "Pursuance Part 3" *John Coltrane A Love Supreme:* MCA/Impulse MCA-5660

Track 14
Jack DeJohnette: "Syzygy" (M. Brecker) *Michael Brecker,* MCA/Impulse MCA-5980

Track 15
Tony Williams: "Moments Notice" (J. Coltrane) *McCoy Tyner Passion Dance:* Milestone M-9091

Track 16
Dave Weckl: "Autumn Leaves" (J. Mercer) *Chick Corea Akoustic Band:* GRP GR-9582